MW01296072

An Ordinary Girl's Dialogue with God

Contrary Action

Wendy Alane Wright

AuthorHouse™
1663 Liberty Drive, Suite 200
Bloomington, IN 47403
www.authorhouse.com
Phone: 1-800-839-8640

First published by AuthorHouse 5/2/2011
Library of Congress Control Number 2008907681
ISBN: 978-1-4389-1248-6

Printed in the United States of America
Bloomington, Indiana
This book is printed on acid-free paper.

To My Parents, William and Judy.
Thank you.
For Giving Me Life.
And For Giving So Much of Yourselves.

Acknowledgements

I wish to acknowledge Desiree Peralta who helped take hundreds of handwritten pages and type it into the computer, getting me started on turning these writings into a book. Desiree I know you were sent by God. Thank you for your ability to read my handwriting when no one else could. Not even me.

I also wish to thank my father for being a life long example of commitment and follow through. Thanks to my four Editors Dr. William D. Wright, Judy Amores, Dr. Jane Hays and Douglass Wright for your brilliant minds! Your thoughts and suggestions were an enormous contribution to this book and it means so much to me that you did it.

I want to thank my brother for being the best brother a sister could ever have, and for loving me all these years, I love you Douglass.

I want to thank Neale Donald Walsh who supported me and told me to just send out my book out even if I didn't have a manager at the time. I also want to thank Depak Chopra and Wayne Dyer for telling the truth, and inspiring the people of this world to greatness. I want to thank all of the musicians, writers, producers and singers who made this CD possible through their amazing talents.

I wish to thank my beloved husband James who believes in me, encourages me and supports everything I do. I love you Golden Lasso.

I wish to thank God. Thank you for speaking to me, and trusting me with sharing your message. Please give me strength to do your will, and to be of service to you in the ways which you have planned.
In all things, Your Will Be Done God, Not Mine.

Table of Contents

SPECIAL THANKS

to all the people along my path who have believed in me,
supported my talents, goals and dreams and have gievn me
opportunities, furthered my abilities and increased knowledge. A life is made of so many people who all contribute to
who you are. I want to thank all of you who have inspired
me.You all have made this Book and my Cds "As I Am," "I
Want Your Love," and "Real Love" possible. Thank you God
1st and foremost for blessing me with talents that have
brought so much peace, joy and happiness to my heart and
to so many others. May I continue to use them in your
Service.

Thank you James T. Smith, Rene van Verseveld, Lee Solt-
ers, Wayne Brady, Lee Kappleman, Mrs. Proto, Mrs. Perry,
Jeff Sydney, Kenny Amorosano, Susan Ferris, Adam Seid,
Johan Rovenstruk, Baldomero Flores, Judith C. Amores,
William Douglass Wright, Jerry Kalajian, Booh Schut,
Anson Williams, Susan Salgado, Bob and Gail Levine, Art
Deco, Tim Redfield, Elisa Fiorillo, Billie Myers, Jeff Trach-
ta, Ronald van Der Meyden, Def La Desh, King Mc, Miker
G, Allan Rich, Steven Cahill, Laura Pallas, Phil McKenna,
Ginny Shields, Pieter Bodegraven, CONTACT INFOR-

Peter Schoonhoven, Karen van Buren, Gerald, Natasha and Ester, Tatjana Simic, Carol Penney, the Alliance Theatre, Bowen Peters Dancing School, Robin Dancy, Diana King, Cathy Smith, Amber Perry, Jane Hays, Marie Lambert, David Cleenewerk, Eric Cleenewerk, Taryn Smith, Richard "Humpty" Vission, Rad Milo, Terry Lippman, Bottlefly, Anna Garcia and Craig, Tamara, Glaze, my vocal students in Holland, Philip Michael Thomas, Ed Wynn, Fred & George, Capital Records Recording School, Denny Seiwell, Liza Minelli, Michael McDonald, Smokey Robinson, Solomon Burke, Michael Schlaifer, Eric Olsen, Jackie & Dez, Billy's Night Out, Cues Bar & Grill, Karen Hudecheck, Una Cassidy, Amber Perry, June Ungureanu, Crystal Waters, my audiences and fans, all the people on radio, VH1, BET and MTV...

and my biggest supporter, my father, Dr. William D. Wright who has encouraged me on, held me when I was falling, and said "I have heard a lot of great singers in my time and Wendy... you are one of the greats."
Thank you Daddy. I love you.

Thank you for sharing your passions, and spirits with me.

MATION

To Contact Wendy Alane Smith

visit www.WAWentertainment.com

To Purchase her Cd's visit www.CDbaby.com

To receive the Contrary Action newsletter

or to buy Wendy Alane Wright's other books

visit the Contrary Action Official Website

at www.ContraryAction.net

As well as Facebook, Twitter and all the social networks.

Contrary Action - INTRODUCTION

- Taking Contrary Action

"Sis quispiam vos have nunquam had you're iens habeo efficio quispiam vos have nunquam perfectus."

"If you want something you have never had, you're going to have to do something you have never done."

Wendy Wright

S even years ago my life was a mess. I was in an abusive relationship. I wasn't accomplishing my goals and I was beating myself up over the mistakes and choices I had made in my life. Today my life is completely different. I have the happiness I had only read about in books, I have a great relationship that movie classics are made of, I have a job I am really good at, get paid well for it and truly enjoy. I feel useful in the world, I am accomplishing my goals and today I love myself deeply for the first time in my life. How did this incredible about face happen in my life? I am no better than anyone else, certainly no stronger.

It all began on November 2, 1999 I was in so much emotional pain about my life that I fell to my knees and cried out to God to please help me. That night a miracle happened that changed my life forever. I had a Divine Intervention from God. He spoke to my Heart. He answered my cry and I became aware of what I was doing in my life that wasn't working. He told me what I needed to do in order to attain the happiness all of us so desperately seek. He explained the purpose of my life, our lives and why we were created. That night He intervened and set me on a completely different path. I had a Divine Intervention.

I wrote down everything I became aware of that

night and for the past five years that I have been in dialogue with Him though Prayer and Meditation. This book contains the answers I had been searching for: Who we really are, Why we are Here, Who is God, How God works, What God wants us to know, How to make our lives and relationships with others work and most importantly: How to have a relationship with God directly.

The purpose of this book is to transform your awareness. To help you express more of who you really are, a loving, creative, awesome human being created by God! The fact is there is nothing wrong with you. You come from God. You come from the source of perfection. You are whole and perfect just the way you are! You have simply been blocking the expression of your true self with fear, old habits, old beliefs and a lack of awareness of WHO YOU REALLY ARE! This book will help you CHANGE some areas in your life that need to be transformed. It is written simply, in a way anyone can understand, no metaphysical mumbo jumbo, although there is nothing wrong with that either!

Where are you in your life right now? It's time to stop and take a real look. Are you the person you want to be? Are you doing what you want to be doing for a living? Do you have a good, healthy relationship with yourself and with others? Do you have a relationship with God that brings you peace?

It's time to take an honest look at ourselves, right Here and right now. Where are you today? Forget the past. Forget what you should have, could have or would have done. Take a moment and decide who you want to be in this moment. Let's start from right Here, right now.

We spend years beating ourselves up for what we've done wrong. We spend years dreaming of what we wish our lives would be like if only... (You fill in the blanks).

Today this book Contrary Action will help you take an honest look at your life and make some of the real changes you have been desiring in your Heart for as long as you can remember.

The concept Contrary Action means taking an action contrary to an action you are currently taking. Or in other words taking different actions than the actions you have been taking up to now.

There is a saying "You can not think your way into right acting. You must act your way into right thinking." It simply means you can think forever about who you want to be and never get there! Only Actions will get you there. This book is about God, Love, and Action.

Think about this. If you keep doing the same thing, you will keep getting the same result. If you want a different result than you have ever had, then you have to do something you have never done before. Makes sense doesn't it? If you want things to change in your life, some things are going to have to change. When we take a Contrary Action we immediately are in the process of achieving a different result! Change is nothing more complicated than that.

If every time you go to the grocery store you buy an orange and eat it. You will be eating oranges forever. If one day you take a Contrary Action and walk past the oranges and buy a banana and eat that, you now have a new experience. Your Contrary Action has lead you to a new result. Change is that simple, Change is about actions. You don't have to figure out what is wrong with you, why your mommy did this or your daddy did that. They had you for 18 years. Whatever you are doing to yourself and your life now, you are doing.

This book is designed to give you "Contrary Actions" you can take that will help you transform your thinking, improve the quality of all of your relationships and ultimately change your life. And guess what? The suggestions in this book work...if you work it.

To "work this book" I mean do what it says! When you get to the Contrary Action section at the end of a chapter, take the action(s) suggested! The actions will change your life, not the reading of this book. Knowledge is fine, but only new action forms new behaviors, which form new habits which form new character. Now don't let the idea of you working this book scare you! It's easy and all it takes is a willingness to try the Contrary Action suggestions one at a time, at your own pace. Take one Contrary Action a year, one a week, or one a day. No matter how many you take, each one will change your life.

Changing your life today, right now, means looking at what is happening in your life right now. What is working what is not working, deciding on some Contrary Actions that you can take and starting to take them one at a time, at your own pace.

Let the messages in this book uplift you, inspire you, and show you what great things are possible when you take Contrary Action and walk ahead through your fears to your goals. My wish for you is the willingness to follow these suggestions in your own life so that you may reach the goals you have for yourself.

Dreaming of being the person we would really like to be is just that, a dream. Being the person we want to be can be a reality. We all make choices in our lives that lead us away from who, what and where we really want to be. Your choice to pick up this book is the first step towards becoming more of the person you know you can be, and creating the life you really want to live!

I am proud of the choice that you have made and honored to be able to share some of the insights I have learned on my journey that have turned my life around.

Are you ready for a Divine Intervention? Take some Contrary Actions!

I Love you all.
May God Bless you.
Wendy Alane Wright

1

PART ONE

Contrary Action -

I

MY DIALOGUE WITH God

*"Operor non incubo preteritus ,
operor non somnium of posterus ,
incumbo mens in tendo moment"*

*"Do not dwell in the past, do not
dream of the future, concentrate the
mind on the present moment."*

**Gautama Siddhartha
(Buddha)**

PART ONE

MY DIALOGUE WITH God

Contrary Action

Chapter 1
- My Beginnings

"Solus res ut sto inter a vir quod quis is volo ex vita , est sepius mereo mos experior is quod fides ut puto is est possible."

"The only thing that stands between a man and what he wants from life, is often merely the will to try it and the faith to believe it is possible."

Richard M. Devos

I have a story to tell you. A story that may be hard for you to believe, but it really happened to me. I had a dialogue with God. I got on my knees one night and cried a primal scream, a scream I had never heard from myself before. I asked God from the depths of my soul for help and He answered me. I had a Divine Intervention. God spoke to me. And I wrote it all down. From that 1st experience and in the five years that have followed, this book has emerged. It contains all the writings I received from God.

How is it possible that God spoke to me? I am not a minister, I am not a preacher. Who am I anyways? I am an ordinary girl born Sept 6, 1966 in Buffalo, New York. It is important for me to tell you what my life was like before I had my Divine Intervention so that you can see that I am just an ordinary girl with ordinary problems, several relationships that didn't work, and an emptiness inside of me from being distant from God.

I was born to an interracial couple in the 60's! My mother is a beautiful white woman and my father is a very handsome, black man, both teachers. My mother has a Masters Degree in Education and my father with a Doctorate who has published numerous books. Both of them intellectuals, very progressive, into equal rights and freedom of choice. They were a beautiful couple, but eventually divorced, leaving my younger brother and I with a broken family at age 12, like so many other American children.

I had a great family. I grew up in a small town in Connecticut from the age of three. My mother ensured I attended dancing school, went camping, visited museums, art galleries, travelled, went to the beach, watched good theatre, played instruments in the marching band and so much more. My mother was very involved with our childhood and instilled in me a great Love and passion for life. She was a very creative parent, always coming up with wonderful things for my brother and I to do. I had good good parents, doing the best they could. I can look back today and say I had a great childhood but it didn't come without pain and challenges.

Being bi-racial, I got made fun of a lot in elementary school and throughout junior high. There were a handful of boys at my schools who called me Nigger, Zebra, Oreo Cookie and Pygmie on a daily basis. Blacks were thought of as less than in those days, and they followed me home from school, throwing berries at me, making fun of me on the bus, and certainly hurting my feelings. I always smiled at them, pretending not to be affected, but I suffered a huge blow to my self-esteem from it. I became very afraid of rejection and overly concerned about what people thought of me.

As a student I was very bright and enjoyed learning but I didn't always pay attention in school. I was preoccupied with talking and trying to be accepted.

My mother introduced me to the theatre when I was 12 and I owe her a debt of gratitude fror ever! In the theatre I was accepted, I was gifted with a lot of talent, and it was a place I fit in, finally! I acted in the Alliance Theatre in New Haven, an award-winning community theater group from the age of 12 to 23 years old. I starred in many plays, acted on a couple of local TV shows, and loved doing the work of an actor. Although I was very gregarious and appeared confident, underneath it all I was shy and uncomfortable in most social situation. I needed to overcome the feelings of insecurity I wore heavily on my sleeve. I needed to fill the hole within me. It was a God-sized hole. But I didn't know that yet.

Adding to my childhood pain, was the fact that my Dad was a workaholic who rarely spent time with me as I grew up. When my brother and I were liuttle children he was more involved, but as we grew he became less and less involved. He was an author and his writing took him away from all of us. By the time I was in my twenties, he had written 41 books and was always in his office writing. It was the reason my mother left him, and his neglect has been the source of one of the deepest pains and challenges in my life. Although I have to say, my Dad is a very kind, loving man who provided extremely well for us. He has always been there for me when I really needed him and I am greatful for that. But the neglect I experienced from him on a daily basis also damaged my self-esteem and my ability to relate with others for years.

So with these two early negative experiences, from mostly men, I had some emotional baggage I had to get through.

In spite of the meanness hurled towards me, I was a kind person. I still cared deeply about people and went out of my way to help others. In my teens and early twenties I did charity work, fed the homeless and spent time with inner city kids mentoring them. Good thing I wasn't mentoring them on relationships! I hadn't figured those out yet. Ha!

I attended Southern Connecticut State University and was on the Dean's List every semester, majoring in Psychology. (I think most Psych majors are really trying to figure themselves out!) I worked on some of my rejection issues in counseling and mustered enough healing and confidence to move to California to pursue my childhood dreams of singing. At 23, a record producer discvovered me in Los Angeles and flew me to Amsterdam where I spent the next four years living with him in Holland writing songs, recording, making records, and traveling through European countries performing. It was awesome! I had several top 20 hit records in Europe and experienced many of my dreams.

But deep down inside I feared rejection and I even feared success. For I felt that if I was really successful, then I wouldn't be the piece of crap I had been told I was, and often believed myself to be. I would be wrong and people don't like to be wrong; even when it is in their best interests!

My relationship with this successful producer lasted for 8 years. In our 4th year of living together we got married. He was a good man, kind and loving to me, very generous and treated me like a queen. We travelled around over Europe, stayed in the nicest hotels, ate in the finest restaurants and I shopped to my heart's content. He believed in all of my musical talents and gave me many opportunities that any singer would dream of. I had many unresolved issues with men and still felt no matter how much he gave, it was never enough to fill the Hole within me. I was busy correcting him and trying to change what

I thought he needed to change about himself. I spent most of our marriage trying to get him to do thing smy way and give me the attention I thought I wasn't getting and never got as a child. I spent years trying to fix what I thought was "wrong" with him, because I never knew how to fix what was wrong with me.

Until my Divine Intervention from God, I tried to fill the void within me by using outside solutions; exercise, substance, sex, travel, shopping, The Forum, Insight Seminars and self-help books. Nothing worked.

Years after my divorce from the producer, I finally met by boyfriend Michel where I experienced even more emotional pain and it finally forced me down on my knees the night I cried out desperately for God's help - and this book began.

Okay so that pretty much tells you what my life was like before my Divine Intervention and dialogue with God. Here I am writing a book about A Divine Intervention from God, that contains writing straight from God. How is that possible?

I am no religious fanatic. I am just an ordinary girl not affiliated with any particular religion. Afterall, I stopped going to church when I was 12 or so. I hadn't ever read the Bible other than a few paragraphs here or there. I owned one but it was in the closet. I had thumbed threw it in hotel rooms and tossed it right back in the drawer. I am not a religious person at all.

So how am I writing a book inspired by God himself? Am I a quack? No. I am just an ordinary girl who discovered one night when I prayed deeply from my heart that God answers. I wrote down everything He said to me that night, and since, and I am telling everybody about it.

What comes in the rest of the pages of this section of the book didn't come from me. You have read about who I was, my insecurities, my unmet needs and self-centered behaviors. I was just an ordinary girl going through life, doing the best I could with what I had until one day God spoke to me. Holy cow!

The night this whole thing happened to me I was laying on the floor crying immersed in my own pity party when evening God Himself broke into my thoughts and interrupted me.

PART ONE

MY DIALOGUE WITH God

Contrary Action

Chapter 2
- Divine Intervention

"Diligo mihi ut EGO minimus mereo mereor is , quoniam ut ut EGO vere postulo it."

Love me when I least deserve it, because that's when I really need it."

Swedish Proverb

It was November 2, 1999, I was in a very tumultuous, unstable relationship with a man named Michel. By my many poor choices after my divorce from the producer, it had been established that my man "picker" was officially broken. My drinking was starting to worry me so I went to get help. I met Michel at an AA meeting in North Hollywood You would be surprised how many famous people are in these LA meetings. He was outside smoking a cigarette like so many addicts who give up drinking and then smoke and drink coffee like fiends.

We started talking. And mind you, this guy was nothing like any guy I would ever go out with. He had tattoos all over his arms called "sleeves" because they covered his arms like the sleeves of a shirt from shoulders to wrists. I had never talked to anyone with Tattoos before. He was absolutely not my "type." So far, my type had been preppy, white New England boys, like the ones that made fun of me and if I got their approval then I would be worth something, temporarily. Still, I noticed this tatooed biker had the prettiest eyes, a beautiful face and looked something like Rob Lowe. I was attracted instantly.

Michel was rebellious, sexy and exciting! From day one we were obsessed with each other of course and I had no balance. As soon as he came into my life most everything else was put on hold - my usual pattern. I didn't spend time with my friends, I constantly avoided success by not following through on some important opportunities and being overly busy with Michel and all his issues. This way I didn't have to ever face my own fears and innadequacies. Same pattern, different man.

During this time, I did four Verizon commercials, sang on more CDs, did backup singing for several major artists, performed in a great live band at many high society events with celebrities, but I was very distracted. I wanted to do more with my talent but I let my disfunctional relationship with Michel take up most of my time and energy, much to my friends and parents dismay. It caused me a great deal of pain to have big dreams inside me and to still be too afraid to really go after them. I was dabling, waiting to see if life was going to walk me like in baseball. This was the third source of the suffering in my life, aggravated by the addiction to unhealthy reliances upon men for my self worth.

Back to him...back to Michel. My co-dependence was off the charts because he was giving me such positive attention. It was like I needed him to function. My friends told me it was an unhealthy relationship and no one liked him but me. People thought he had a negative energy around him. My brother called it a black cloud. I didn't see it that way. No one could see him the way I did; how he would get out of the car to help an elderly person across the street, how he could greet people in over 20 languages or how amazing it was to watch him paint his canvases for hours as he created spectacular works of art.

Well me, all I could see was his smile, his beautiful eyes and the wonderful way he made me feel. His attention to me was what I lived for. I truly believed it would make up for all the damage in my life and fill the void within me. In this case I staked my life on it. My mother was deeply afraid he was going to kill me during one of his violent outbursts.

Michel was a recovering drug addict who admitted he had a lot of problems and couldn't stay sober for more than one year. (red flag.) I met him sober so I had not experienced his drug use or the irratic behavior of a using addict. My gosh I had no idea what I was in for.

Sober Michel and I had been together everyday for nine months and we were absolutely infatuated with eachother.He was lots fun to be with, we went to movies, to the beach, he made me picnics and drew bubble baths for me when I came home from work. We had so much fun together, we laughed so hard we cried. I had more fun with him than I had ever had with anyone else in my life. He spent time, lots of time with me, which was my biggest requirement for a man. In fact, Michel always wanted to be with me, night and day. I defined all of this as "Love."

Sober Michel was tremendously romantic and shared his deepest feelings with me. He talked openly with me and took a deep interest in me. Most importantly he was not neglecting me. He came to every band rehearsal, every performance, every gig I did and was very supportive. He "Loved" the ground I walked on, literally. He would put rose petals from my parking space all the way to my front door so I could walk on them. He packed my lunch for work everyday and cooked me breakfast every morning. He gave me beautiful cards saying the things my heart longed to hear. I was head over heels in "Love." The romance was amazing and isn't this what every woman is looking for?

But what about the three pages of red flags I wrote about him? I choose to overlook them. Why do people overlook red flags? I think the reason is we are all so desperate to be Loved we don't want to see people for who they really are. We want to see them for who we "hope they will be."

Michel he was highly irresponsible. He got violent sometimes. He didn't call when he said he would. He sometimes just didn't show up for days at a time. One of my girlfriends said he was using drugs. I didn't believe her. He always had a story for being 3-4 hours late like one of his friend's cars broke down or he slept through the alarm. (He slept through a lot of alarms!) But his stories didn't sit right with me and it seemed he had a lot of friends with broken down cars. yes, there was something seriously off about him, I knew it in my gut and it bothered me, but I continued to overlook the red flags.

Everyone around me was telling me to leave him, that he wasn't good for me, that I needed to focus on myself and my career and just leave men alone for awhile. I had gone from one relationship to another but I wasn't listening. I didn't want to lose his Love. Hmmm...His "Love. Was that Love? More like, I didn't want to lose his attention, his affection or the illusion of Love.

One day he dissapeared for a week. Suddenly he started calling me late at night high on drugs with girls in the background, telling me he didn't need me, he had someone else. I cried hysterically almost everyday that week and at the end of the week he got sober again, got on his hands and knees and begged me to take him back. He promised to stay sober. I believed him. I wanted to.

For another year we carried on. We watched movies in bed, picnics on the beach, talking and laughing for hours.

He gave me flowers everyday and we made Love morning, noon and night. With time I was even more become dependant on him for my feelings of self worth. I was using his approval and attention like a drug and still over-looking every red flag.

Another dissapearance and this time when he called in the middle of the night high on drugs, he said he was watching me and he had a gun and if I went out with anyone else he would kill me. He stalked me for weeks. I was in emotional pain like I had never been before in my entire life. I didn't know how to get out of this relationship. My issues with men had me so messed up. I missed the sober Michel that I Loved who was kind and loving to me. Within a week or two he got sober again, got on his knees begged me to take him back and I did. This cycle went on for 2 1/2 years.

I was worth more than this. I wasn't raised this way. I was a college educated girl, from a good family in Connecticut, raised by upper level educators. Geez, how on earth did I get caught up in a relationship with a drug addict?

One day after Michel had six months of sobriety again, he kissed me in the morning and told me he Loved me deeply and said I was the greatest thing that had ever happened to him. He appreciated how much I loved him and thanked me for believing in him and gving him another chance with me. He said would do whatever it took to stay sober so we could keep our wonderful life together. He patted me playfully on the buttt, hugged me and we went our separate ways to work.

I didn't hear from him that night, or the next night or the following week, or the next 5 weeks! He just disappeared. This time my heart was broken because I had maintained so much faith and hope for us. This time I was devastated. I truly didn't know what to do anymore. I didn't know if he was dead or alive and I had become so co-dependant on him I could hardly function without him. I was in agony, an agony I had never known before. I felt like I was going to die. I didn't know where to turn or what to do.

So one night when the pain of loss got bad enough, I finally dropped to my knees on my living room floor and a cry came out of me that sounded primitive. I cried to God and told him how much pain I was in. I begged him from the depths of my heart to please help me. I said LOVE me God, "Hold me." I needed a hug so badly right now. I wanted God to wrap his arms around me and surround me in his Love. It was the first time I had ever called for God like that.

Suddenly, the thought popped into my mind to get up and put in "SynchroDestiny," the Depak Chopra tapes I had been listening to recently. I said to myself what a good idea, that's a positive thought. It'll get me moving in the right healing direction.

I got up and while walking across the room to get the tape, I started hearing a few more suggestions. I can't remember what they were, but I said to myself wait a minute, this sounds important, I've got to write these things down. I didn't know at that moment if it was me saying these things to myself, or my subconscious or what, but I knew I needed to sit down and write nonetheless.

I began writing, without thinking about the words that were coming out. I was writing so fast my hand could barely keep up with the words that were coming to me. The words were popping into my head and I was putting them down on paper.

I didn't know what the words were until after the letters left my pen and even then the information was coming so fast I didn't have time to read what I had written nor even think about what it had meant. I just had to keep scribbling because there was more coming and I needed to keep up. At this point I knew I was being moved by something to write, so I didn't interfere in any way. I just kept writing with a fervor. At one moment I thought that God was maybe talking to me, but I just kept writing.

After writing 20 or so pages I stopped to read back through what I had just written. I couldn't believe my eyes. I had just been told very specific information regarding my life, my choices, my relationship with Michel and what my true purpose on this planet was. I was reading things I had known all along but refused to accept or act on. Words so honest, so true, so contrary to what I was doing I knew it couldn't have come from me. This first entry on the next page is what God said to me directly. Although very personal, I will share it with you.

WHAT GOD SAID TO ME THAT NIGHT:

I want You to realize, You can only count on You to give you what You need. That You must turn to me in all matters big and small and through me and my will You will find salvation and your true direction. Hurt not little one because I am holding You against my breast. I am cradling You in the palms of my hands with such

LOVE and tenderness even You do not know, nor can You imagine.

I have told You time and time again, let go of all else but me, Yourself, the gift I have given You. Fly high with your talent and You will be free. You will see that is the only way You will go in the right direction. That is the road to your true purpose and joy.

Your true purpose has not to do with men. It is not to do with belonging to a man. It is not to do with relationship with men. It is not to do with your feelings about men. These are limited, shallow distractions from your soul's sole purpose.

Let go of them. They are not your calling. See higher. Let yourself transcend to a higher level of your soul. Be willing to let go. Let go of the pain. Let go of the blame. Let go of the fear. Let go of the doubt. Let go of trying to control. Let go of people. Let go of trying to fix on anything or anyone. Let go of strange human entanglement.

You are a glorious child of God, whom I have brought forth from the clouds to shine down on this earth the radiant light of God.

Shine my light child like You have never

shined before and You will be okay. You will be free. You will be with Me.

Don't doubt me child, as I have never doubted You. You see the road, the path, yet You constantly set up road blocks. You know in your heart that I am with You and I am leading You exactly where You need to go, but You keep fighting me.

Why do You resist so child? Let go. Know me. Let me show You. Let me LOVE You. Let me help You LOVE yourself. You need no one, save me and yourself. You think You do but You don't. You are my messenger, my child. I have instilled a gift in You a voice that is not yours to hoard. It is for You to shine.

I have placed You like a beacon of light on the earth and in your ego and fear You are constantly trying to hide, dim or abandon your light. Stop. Let it shine. That is your sole purpose for your life, to let my light in You shine.

You know and have always known. You are not one to get wrapped up in material things or worldly matters, but matters of the heart. However You think your salvation is in matters of the heart with a few men here and there. Your salva-

tion is in matters of the heart of global propor-tions, worldwide LOVE. Giving and sharing your gift on the greatest level, is the answer for You. Through that You will magnify who You are 10 times and be filled by your own light.

Others cannot fill You. You have misjudged that. Yet try and try You may, You will never re-ceive joy in that manner. You will never receive wholeness from people. You will never heal your heart or find peace in people, only in God and only by giving your gift to the world, as I have intended.

How long You struggle is up to You, for I have made the road so easy for You. I have opened ev-ery door because my purpose for You is clear. Ac-cept, trust and have faith in that purpose, in the source of that purpose. Go forward down the path I have set for You and watch many miracles be-fall You and others. You will not find pain on this Road Wendy. You will find joy and You will be okay with that.

You think You need your pain. You think your pain is who You are. You are afraid to let go of the pain because You think You will not know yourself anymore. You are afraid of who You will become.

Trust me that You will be alright. You will be more than You ever dreamed possible and You will be okay. You can handle this. You will feel safe and You will feel like You did as a child on a brisk autumn day in Connecticut, when everything was alright. That's truly the worse you will ever feel.

Trust me child, I have no purpose in steering You wrong. You are calling me for help for answers and as always I am here with You, giving You what You need to hear and know. Once again and always I will You give You what You need. But You must take the actions, You must make the choices.

You are my Beloved and I will tell You as often as You need to hear. Open your wings and fly freely. Attach to no one and nothing. They only hold You down and imprison You. Fly freely like a bird flies the earth. Rejoice in giving Yourself to all, nay to one. Enjoy the brightness of your light and know that You are doing God's work with your life.

Don't constrict Yourself. Don't be constricted by others. Spend very little time in human relations and all your quality time in God.

I have given you a gift that even You sometimes doubt, but do not doubt the power of God. You know not what I have in store for You and your gift. Only be assured it is greater and more wonderful than You can possible imagine and You will not know how it will all turn out or manifest.

All You must do is be free. Move freely and be willing to go where I lead You. I Love You Wendy my child. You are one child I am very proud of and have high purpose for. There are those I select to carry messages in certain manners and I have selected You, as You have always known, to carry me through your light, your laughter, your LOVE, your beauty and your voice.

Sing like a bird. Exhault and up lift me. Sing the praises of beauty and joy. Sing of Laughter and LOVE. Let people see how truly magnificent they are and can be. Let them see their own light through You. Give your light to them as a gift to brighten their hearts and souls, to give them hope and to touch them with me. Know that your pur-

pose here is greater than You have imagined or have allowed Yourself to see or accept.

After reading this I cried deeply. I cried about what God had said to me. This writing was very personal to me. His intervention addressed exactly what was going on in my life. What my deepest pains and troubles were. It got my attention. I know if you are on your knees openly talking to God he is going to address your pains and your concerns in life.

I knew that what I had written was God talking to me and telling me His will for me because His suggestions were absolutely NOT what I had been doing with my life. In fact, I was doing the exact opposite. All my life I've done things "my way," self destructive things that were not loving to myself, and have sometimes hurt others. Things a loving God would never intend for me. Somewhere inside myself I knew that, but I didn't want to listen to anybody else and I had a difficult time following the voice deep within me that tried to steer me in a better direction. I now know that voice was God and that voiceis in all of us.

No, like many people I always wanted everything my way, which never worked. I also thought if people would just do things the way I wanted them to that I would be alright. In fact I used to think that I had been given the only copy of the book with all the answers in it, and if everyone else would just do as I said the world would be okay. It's ironic now that I have written a book with answers, but they are God's answers, not mine. What a difference!

I was self-will out of control. I had never surrendered to God's Will. I didn't even know what God's will was anyways. Was it what I had heard in church as a child? Was it religion? And if so which religion? According to David Barrett et al, editors of the "World Christian Encyclopedia: A comparative survey of churches and religions - AD 30 to 2200, "there are 19 major world religions which are subdivided into a total of 270 large religious groups, and many smaller ones." Which one was the right one? Would I find the answers in a mosque, a temple, synagogue, or shrine?

The fact was I had no idea that God could fill the void inside me. I didn't know where to begin to look for God, or that aligning my deepest self with God was the Answer. I knew of God but I didn't know God.

At that point in my life I thought: who was God anyway? I couldn't see him. He didn't live next door. Why should I turn my will over to something I couldn't prove existed? I was agnostic. Besides what was His Will? What the Bible said? The Koran? Torah? Talmud? Qur'an & Ha-

dith? The Tripitaka? The Veda? Tao-te-Ching? The Book
of Mormon? I had no idea what God's will was. Too many
people's conflicting stories had left me confused.

I had no idea that God was simply Love and that he
lived inside me and that He is my highest self. That all I
had to do was sit quietly and I would find God. That If I
acted from Love I would be in God's will. I was afraid that
"turning my will over to God" actually meant "losing" myself somehow. I didn't understand at the time that it actually meant "finding" myself.

So back to that night of my Divine Intervention. I
looked at what I had written and the handwriting was very
difficult to read. Something inside me said I have more to
write, it's not time to stop. So I wrote another 18 pages.
After I had finished that I decided I had better record what
I had written into a tape recorder, because when I looked
at the writing it was so difficult to read. I knew if I didn't
do it quickly I would never be able to recognize the words
at a later date.

I recorded those 38 pages into my tape recorder and
afterwards I just couldn't believe what I was reading. I became excited and amazed. Energy was going through my
body and I didn't know what to do. I felt restless, like I
needed to get up and do something, like take a shower or

something. But I was still being guided by something inside me that told me to keep writing.

After writing many more pages and doing more recording, I got up and started walking around. I couldn't believe that God was talking to me. Doubt began to fill my mind. I asked out loud, "How do I know for sure I am talking to you God?" All of a sudden another thought crossed my mind to look under the notebook I had been writing in. I saw a tape lying directly underneath it that came from a church I occasionally attended called AGAPE Spiritual Center of Truth in Culver City, California led by Dr. Reverend Michael Beckwith. You may remember him from the book and movie, "The Secret."

I listened to various Agape tapes sometimes at home because they made me feel good. I always heard something positive at Agape and felt a very loving energy there. I believed in it's principles of peace, oneness, unity and what "Agape" stood for – "unconditional Love." However, I knew I was not always the living, walking embodiment of these things in my relationships. I believe Michael Beckwith is one of those people that Walks the Talk. But I was not at that level. I had not surrendered to God's Will as a result of going to Agape or any other church in my life. My life was not working and my demons were still destroying me.

Anyway, I was very surprised to see the tape there and don't remember putting it there. A thought came to me to put the tape in the player. I knew immediately that finding the tape was no coincidence and that if I listened, there would probably be something very specific I would hear that would apply exactly to what was going on in that room at that moment. I know the universe works this way, it's called synchronicity or coincidences. Things don't happen by accident– this much I knew.

We have all have experienced these seeming coincidences. For example, you think about someone you haven't see in a long time and wonder how they are doing. All of a sudden you run into them or they call you out of the blue. On another occasion, you may not know what to do about something, you're really upset so you go sit in the park to think and by "coincidence" someone sits down next to you who happens to have gone through the exact same thing you are going through and they share their experience with you and it helps. Coincidence? No. Unexplainable? Yes. But I say it's God talking to you through other people, guiding you and helping you on your journey.

Now I had just asked God how could I be sure it was Him I was talking to. Now be ready for this because this is going to blow your mind. The tape was in the middle, not rewound. I hit play and this is exactly what was said:

"Communion means that something goes out & something returns. That we not only seek God, but find God. There is no such thing as a one-sided communion. Unless the response is there, the attempt to hold communion ends in loneliness and futility. We must gain the assurance that God not only hears, but he answers. That we are not talking in a vacuum or attempting to commune with the emptiness of space. Jesus said that all space is filled with the divine presence, peopling itself with the many forms of its own creation. He taught that all things and people are rooted in this divine intelligence and because it is individualized in each, it is personal to all."

I stopped the tape and sat in disbelief on my living room floor. Laughing, crying. I could not believe my ears. The tape could have been about anything, any subject under the sun that is constructable by the human language. But it simply wasn't. It said, "We must gain the assurance that God not only hears, but HE answers."

After hearing that and reading the words on the pages I had written, I had no more doubt. I knew that God was speaking directly to me. What I was writing were his answers to my call, and absolutely, they were the words of God. There was an intelligence in his word that went exceeded mine and there was an ability to see the truth went beyond my ability. There was a peace in his words that gave me comfort. I believe when people hear the truth they know it. Over the course of the next five years I have prayed and called to God and He has answered and I have written down everything he has said to me. This book is some of what I have learned from each of those moments or "Sessions with God."

All the words in this book were given to me, but they are also for You; for Divine Intelligence "may be individualized in each" but it is personal to all. This book is for all of us, we human beings on this planet seeking our purpose and struggling with the many issues we are confronted with and trying our best to understand.

What God wants me to tell you directly, His words are in italics. They came out of a five-year journey that began that night on November 2, 1999 when I fell to my knees and begged God to help me and I had what some people call...a Divine Intervention.

What God Told Me To Tell You:

Don't get so bogged down in the pain. The drama of poor me. You are so self-pitying. Open your hearts to the glory of who You truly are and the gifts that life is constantly giving you. Remember You have so much LOVE to give and your life can touch someone in the most special way. LOVE yourself. There is so much to LOVE.

Sometimes it's so easy to get into self-hate and self-blame, but life's too short for that. Let go of your self-loathing. He Loves You and wants You to LOVE yourself.

Nothing You have done makes you unlovable, just lost and misguided from Him to various extremes. He has created no one, save in His image and even your worst moments are His creation. Your worst flaws are inspired by His original creation. You have invented nothing. God has invented all.

Turn yourself over to the vision God has of You. Let go of your vision based on appearances and your judgements of right and wrong. God has a greater measuring scale. Yours is broken and inconsequential. Don't waste precious time of your life misdiagnosing yourself. Let God's diagnosis of You be all You need to know.

So many times in life, you struggle trying to make life what you think it should be. You try to make things go the way you think they should go. You are trying to play God in your own lives and when it all goes wrong you are shocked and amazed at the outcome. You are sometimes even devastated by the turn out. This comes from a lack of faith and trust in God. He has your best interests in mind at all times. He sees the bigger picture.

Stop trying to manipulate life according to your ideas of what you "think" you need. Rather, ask God what He would have you do on any given day, in any given circumstance.

God works in the strangest and most miraculous ways. He is working even when You think He is not, when everything points to Him abandoning you He is working for You. Even when it looks like things are going "wrong" for You. Then low and behold everything makes sense again and You think, oh is that what God had in mind?

You can't always measure or understand what God is doing. You don't have the equipment. Just as You can not see radio waves or microwaves with the naked eye but You know they are there. You only have thoughts and perceptions of God which usually come from an extremely limited place. You think in terms of human possibilities and You are trying to say that God is only capable of human possibilities.

The truth is God is capable of anything. God is grand. God is all and all is possible in God. Doubt not God's intentions for You, because they will always manifest in your best interests. If You let God guide You, life will be the heaven You are looking for. Do You know the gold at the end of the rainbow, the jackpot You have been waiting to hit is already here for You? You've already won it! You just have to claim your prize.

PART ONE

MY DIALOGUE WITH God

Contrary Action

Chapter 3
-   Asking God for Answers

"Congruo est vox nos utor ut nos can't animadverto campester quod traho."

Coincidence is the word we use when we can't see the levers and pulleys.

Emma Bull

I was laying on the beach one day and longing to be closer to God, but I didn't know how at that time. I asked outloud; God, Universe show me the way to you. I don't know which religion is the truth, I don't know if its Buddhism, Christianity, Judaism. All I ask is for is the truth and the truthful path. Whatever the truth is, that is what I will embrace.

A few days later I received a call about the classified Ad I had placed looking for a roommate. I forgot to specify female only, so a man called and somewhere along the line, the conversation steered toward God. He was a Christian, reborn and was convinced that if I didn't do God's Will I was going to hell. I had very little tolerance for that conversation, because it is my belief that hell is where you are when you don't do God's will but it is not Eternal and God certainly doesn't put you there, We do, that is until we surrender to God's way of life and Will.

Well, this Bible thumper said if I didn't believe that Jesus Christ was God's only son I was going to hell. I said what about the children that are born in Africa in the jungle and have never heard of Jesus Christ are they going to Hell? He said yes.

Thinking for a moment that if I was a parent, would I put my children in hell for eternity for making mistakes or not saying magic words? No, because I Love my children and want their happiness, not their damnation. It wouldn't make any sense. If God is Love, what is loving about that? Think about your own children, Would you do that do them? Then why would God who is greater and more loving and forgiving than we do such a thing or want such a thing to be done. Further, as Christ was being crucified on the cross he said "Forgive them father for they know not what they do." According to Christianity the whole point of Jesus was to allow forgiveness for all of us. It was so important to God that we learn the lesson of forgiveness that he sacrificed his son to teach it to us. He made the lesson dramatic, and never forgettable.

Yet on the other side of that same coin we are supposed to believe that God is inconsistent in his forgiveness and in fact has no forgiveness for some and will put them in hell for eternity. What things then does he forgive and not forgive? I don't buy this belief. If God values forgiveness that much I am sure he extends it to all people and all things. Even those who are not "saved" in the Christian sense of the word. This is a hard thing for many people to accept because of their limited ability to forgive. They automatically assume God has those same human limitations. God Loves us all, forgives us all and wants happiness and joy for us all. There are many religions around the world, forms and expressions of spirituality, all leading to God. That is truth for me.

Well, back to my story, of this Bible thumper. He called for a couple days in a row, speaking of Jesus and the devil and hell, and I said you know what, this conversation is pointless. We are too far apart in our thinking to even discuss this. I won't see your way, you won't see mine. So I bless you, wish you God's perfect peace, take care and goodbye.

For days I was shaken by the calls and I shared with a friend that I was confused because everything he said went against my beliefs. But I remembered laying on the beach the previous week asking God for the truth and out of the blue I get this call about Jesus. Well, no other religious representatives called; no Mulsims, Jews, Hindus, Mormons, etc. So I wondered what God was trying to tell me about the Bible and Jesus. I knew hell and damnation wasn't the answer but I was open to hearing more. After all, God can't talk to me if I think I have heard all I will ever hear from him. If I already think I know Him He can't reveal anything new to me. So I kept myself open to information that may come my way. I honestly believe if you ask for answers you will receive them.

The following week I was having a discussion with my girlfriend Chantal, about my destructive relationship with Michel. I told her how unhealthy it was and honestly shared with her that some of my behavior with Michel and other past relationships with men that were destructive.

She shared with me that she used to be exactly like that, and I was shocked because she seemed so kind and peaceful now. I was definitely interested in what happened to her, how she changed. I longed to change too. So I asked her how she had changed and she said Jesus came into her life and changed her. I remarked: "no way." She told me she used to be very angry and vengeful but she found Jesus.

Because I Loved and trusted her and I wanted the peace that she had, I was open to going to her church with her; even though I did not believe that Jesus was the only way and that the Bible is the only communication from God to be revered on the whole planet.

I sat in the church with my arms crossed and a closed heart, because I just didn't believe. I wasn't willing to listen. But I remembered that it was important for me to listen as I had so recently learned. So I closed my eyes and asked God, praying silently to please open my heart, because as long as it was closed I wouldn't hear what he wanted to me to hear there.

At the end of my prayer, I opened my eyes and sitting directly in front of me a few rows up I recognized a boy Philip Nabors that I knew from 3,000 miles away back in a very small town in Connecticut called Hamden, where I went to elementary school with him. He was one of my best little friends and I hadn't seen him in 15 or 20 years. Can you believe it? I burst into tears and my heart opened up and was filled with Love. It was no accident Phil Nabors was sitting directly in front of me, or that I saw him at that moment. I prayed to God to open my heart. He used Philip to do so.

What you don't know, and why this "coincidence" was so significant to me, is that this boy was extremely important to me as I was growing up. I was the only black and white child in my school and he was one of the 5 other black kids in a 95% white school. He defended me when kids would pick on me, stand up for me and protect me. He was very special to me, Philip saved my spirit many times. God picked a messenger very close to my heart.

When I saw him I could feel my heart had opened wide; as I had asked God to do, and I cried tears of joy. God opened my heart all right using the universe to communicate with me once again by bringing to me this friend I Loved from school. You see that is how God works. We are not alone in this universe. God is an intelligent and creative loving Being who always wants our growth and wants us to reach a deeper understanding of Him and ourselves.

With my heart open that day, I was able to listen in that church to the message of Love and God's Way. It was amazing and afterwards I talked to my long- lost friend and he introduced me to his beautiful wife and their 2 children and I was so happy for him and so happy to see him.

I was so moved by the experience which other people might call a simple coincidence, I do not. Chantal asked me to join her Bible group and I said yes. I studied with them for several months. The group included the most wonderful women; Lucy, her husband was the minister of the church, Larese who sang with James Brown and Chantal. I attended their church functions and BBQ's and this greatly increased my commitment to God, for which I am ever thankful. I have never steered off the path of God since. And I have to thank those strong, beautiful women for their Love and support, their patience in answering my never-ending stream of questions and most of for messagers of God's Will and Love for us all.

Eventually I stopped going to that Christian re-born Bible study because some of the concepts were simply not acceptable to me and were not consistent with what I had been hearing from God directly. And nothing they said or did could get me past these discrepancies.

For example, they believed the Bible says that homosexuality is a sin and those people will go to hell. The Bible specifically says,"Do you not know that the wicked will not inherit the kingdom of God? Do not be deceived: Neither the sexually immoral, nor idolaters, nor adulterers, nor male prostitutes, nor homosexual offenders, nor thieves, nor the greedy, nor drunkards, nor slanderers, nor swindlers will inherit the kingdom of God. (NIV, 1st Corinthians 6:9-11)

I simply do not believe God is against homosexuals. We are all God's children, Loved equally by Him and created by Him in His image... no exceptions. And God is a loving God not a punishing one, not a hell and damnation God. I believe if men are born with more female chromosomes making them more feminine and attracted to men they can't help it, it's nature. And why would God put his own creations in hell? Doesn't in fact God Love diversity? Or otherwise he would have created only one kind of flower, one kind of plant, one kind of tree, one kind of animal or one kind of person.

I don't know if Jesus was God's "only" son. I think he

was. So far my opinion of Jesus is that he was truly committed to God's Will beyond any human being I've ever heard
about, and I humble myself before him because of that. He
may be God's only son, I believe he may be supernatural. I
certainly don't know this for sure, does anyone? That's why
it's called faith. I do believe Jesus was the great example
of what human beings can be. He was a great teacher and
it seems no other human has had that kind of commitment
to God before or since then. Certainly no one has replicated
his kind of impact on the world.

But I simply do not believe that people in other religions who have surrended to God and live a peaceful, har-
monious and loving life are going to hell for eternity because they don't recognize Jesus as the "only" son of God.
And nothing in God's writings to me have ever said anything about that. But for sure, if Jesus is the only Son of
God, then I am okay with that too. For me I have taken
Christ into my heart and believe him the Son of God who
died on the cross for my sins. But it is above my pay grade
to tell anyone else that Christ is the only way to God.

I do say whatever the truth is, God please reveal it to
me, I am open. The difference is I will not spend my life arguing with people about something we just don't know for
sure. This fight about who is right or wrong keeps people

from practicing the teachings of Christ, from practicing the Love of Christ. They call themselves Christians yet don't act like Christ. So instead, I try to follow Jesus's examples of how he lived his life and I treat people lovingly in all the things I do. It is said Christ was loving, forgiving, kind and a servant to others, placing himself last and others first. It is so easy for people to call themselves Christians and then engage in behavior that contradicts Christianity.

I created a T-Shirt it says on the front "You call yourself a Christian?" and on the back it says ..."So start acting like Christ." You can buy it on my website www.contraryaction.net

Anyway, even though I hadn't fully embraced Jesus as the "only" way and the Bible the "only" truth on this planet, that prayer that day on the beach led me to a deeper relationship with God, which is exactly what I had prayed for. It led me on an entirely different path. It led me to searching, questioning and reading many comparative religion books and finally to an understanding that prayer and meditation and God's Will are "the" way of every religion on this earth. Every religion...Buddhism, Christianity, Catholicism, Hinduism, etc. It's says so in The Upanishads, The Koran, The Talmud, The Bible etc, etc. It is the one similarity in all religions. And for me it is the truth. The truth for me is that I get on my knees and ask God directly what His Will for me is and ask him for the power, strength and courage to carry that out. That's all! No arguing about whose truth is more truthful.

So my deepeer path towards God was defined by a series of experiences that I would not have predicted, but was open enough to explore. We don't always know what God has in mind concerning the big picture. But if our heart is open and we are willing, He will lead us to where He wants us to be. have faith and trust in God.

I have had many experiences in my life, where God has used books, people and the universe in general to communicate with me, and some people called them God Shots which is the name of my next book. Depak Chopra calls it Synchronicity. Many downplay these things and say, "oh that was just a coincidence." I say God is talking to me and yes it freaks me out sometimes. But I wonder if it happens to everyone. I think so, only you have to be listening fori t.

God speaks to all of us all the times. Do we tune in and listen? That is the ultimate question. There are those of us that do receive the joy we are seeking and those of us that don't. Some continue to struggle through life until they surrender to God's Will. When I say God's Will I don't mean your community's belief of God's Will for you or your religious group's belief of God's Will for you - I mean God's direct Will for you that only you can hear when you are in prayer and meditation with Him. His Will for you is personal. The specifics of His Will for you may differ from the specifics of his Will for another.

That is just the way of the universe, because, remember, you are not in control. He is and He sets up this thing called "Life," not you. He set up the perameters, the rules, the way it works. You can either listen to how it works and live by it or you can spend your lifetime trying to impose your own rules on His game and suffer. How futile and vain is that way of spending a life? A lifetime which God has so gloriously mapped out for you to experience with pleasure, joy, peace, happiness and abundance.

Another experience of God providing me with answers occurred while I was writing this very book. I was having yet another problem with a man I kept insisting on being with, although it was clearly not God's intention for me to be with him. I was at my computer typing this manuscript and I got very tired all of a sudden. I had learned in a communication seminar previously in my life, that if we are listening to something and all of a sudden get very tired, it is our mind's ways of trying to shut out the information, trying to avoid the truth. It is at those moments we need to listen even more intently to what we were told.

So I looked at what I had just been writing "Often when given a piece of the puzzle, the first thing we should do rather than try and interpret it with our limited abilities is ask God what it means and what God would like us to do."

I got up and tried to escape to the TV but it wouldn't turn on, for no apparent reason. It was plugged in. I took it as a sign. I said "Fine God, what does this crisis with my boyfriend mean and what am I supposed to do here?"

I thought to myself and these powerful insights came to me, "He is not the one for you. This relationship doesn't work. Focus on you. Concentrate on your talents and doing with them what you know you should do." I said to myself, I better go sit down with the pen again, looks like God is ready to take me to school. I was right and the following message is more about all of us and how we keep trying to live our lives guided by our own self-serving EGOS. We keep doing the same things and expecting different results. That is the definition of insanity. <u>The following passage God wanted me to deliver this message as a wake up call for all of us. He said:</u>

"Once again you have tried to manipulate the circumstances in your life to suit what You think You need.

How did it turn out? Did You experience more joy or more pain? Did You experience peace or pain? Did You experience Love or pain? Did You experience a higher version of Yourself or a lack of Love for Yourself?

Were your actions considerate and loving or were they manipulative and controlling? Did life flow with ease and great health or did You experience confinement and restriction? Did You feel goodness or pain? Did You experience a truthful, calm state of well being or chaos and destruction?

It matters not how you try to manipulate your life, My Will for you will always be victorious in the end. I Am in control. I Am in the driver's seat and you can do nothing without Me.

It is My Will you will eventually end up following, whether it is in this lifetime, or the one to follow. You will always come back to Me because I Am the road, I Am the light, I Am the door, I Am the path to your salvation. You cannot live a full and truly purposeful life without finding out what purpose I have for you. You must and You all will eventually come to Me.

How much destruction you cause Yourself, others and your entire planet is completely up to You. How much time you spend in pain and confusion is ultimately up to you. I Am constantly showing you the door, You are forever turning a deaf ear and a blind eye.

Hear Me not if you will. It is up to you who will suffer and it is not My intention for you to suffer, but I have given You free will. Freedom to choose your actions and your thinking at any time. I have given you the power to create as I have it and one day you will learn the true nature of who You are and will honor it. I can not force you to give up inflicting pain upon yourself as You can not force a drug addict to give up drugs.

You must determine for Yourself the truth of who You are and how you choose to live. You must recognize the glory inside of You as I have placed it. You must want the gifts I am trying to give You. You must want the peace, joy, Love and harmony I have placed before You.

I can not force feed your inheritance to You nor can I convince You of your merit. You must realize these things for Yourself.

Oh, how it pains Me to see You struggle and there is nothing I can do except steer You in the right way with My little signs and encouragements or coincidences. But You inevitably are determining the outcome of your experience.

I can only say please do not fight Me so hard. I have

your best interests at heart my children. I LOVE you. I cre-ated You. I want You to experience Yourself in your fullest glory.

A painter does not pick up a brush and paint part of a picture. A painter wants to see their painting in all its finished glory. A rose does not open halfway. A rose opens fully to achieve its fullest glory. It is its destiny.

So too it is for You. Your purpose is to open fully to your fullest potential, experiencing Yourself in your fullest glory. That is your nature. That is my purpose for You. I created You thus.

You can not recreate yourself into something else, as a rose can not recreate itself into a lamb. Spiritual enlight-enment, ever unfolding into your fullest glory is the true nature of your being. You will continue to struggle with acceptance of that as long as You do.

Realize it is your ego that hinders your journey: your self-doubt and your false grandiosity, the ego's defining characteristics. Your ego was made to guide you to Me, not to hinder or imprison You.

Stop misinterpreting its use in your life! You have been given an internal compass. Use it. When You are act-ing in ego, You are not acting in God, You are not acting in LOVE. You should not be acting in ego, it is a tool not a place to act from. You should be acting from your heart and letting the ego show You when You are and when You aren't.

My children, I am not a cold, unloving God. I have never forsaken You. Why do You judge Me so? I am only here to LOVE You, guide you, help You. Why have You so forsaken Me? Have I not given You every precious thing I can think of? Have I not given You every opportunity imaginable? Will You let the cruel or self-centered actions of others make You doubt Me or My sheer existence?

Why, when one of You murders another You think there can be no God?

Why, when You humans have a country that is starving because You do not feed each other do you say there is no God? If there was a God people wouldn't be starving. Have I not given You enough food to feed the world? Have You not created enough technology to feed the world? Why do You choose not to?

Why is it when You perceive Yourself disconnected from Me and find Yourselves filled with hate and fear do You point Me as the cause of your wars?

Have I not given You a heart, a Soul and a Mind to interpret life? Are You not making choices about how to behave, who to Love and whether or not to LOVE Yourself?

I Am not to blame.

Free will is just that, FREE WILL. You can choose at anytime who You are going to be on this planet. You can choose at any time whether You come from LOVE or Hate. When one of You chooses to act in an unloving manner, why am I to blame?

Hitler murders millions of people, assisted by hundreds more and I Am to blame for their choices? You say "If there was a God how could this happen? How could God let this happen."

Are You saying it was a mistake to give You free choice? That I should not let You roam the earth uncovering it's beauty, magic and many mysteries, ever unfolding as you stumble upon them?

Should I have placed you in a dark box and left You there for the duration of your life and given You only a few toys to play with? Yet You blame Me for everything. For giving You everything. Why do you hate Me so? Why do You hate Yourselves so?

I gave You freedom of choice because I LOVE You. Because I trust You. Because I want everything for You. I want You to experience all the Joy, beauty, LOVE and happiness life has to offer. Why blame Me when You only have Yourselves to blame?

Oceans, gravity, earthquakes, tornadoes, floods, sometimes the earth heaves and shoves. It is a planet floating in space with a thousand systems working at once. Many of You are caught up in their movements and a physical death is the result. It is not a spiritual death - yet this you do not understand.

You have interpreted the pain of death as proof that there is no God. How could God let us die this way or that way? If I had associated pleasure with death would you have still made the same conclusion?

You associate pleasure with God and Pain with No God. Therefore, You are always questioning my existence. Yet I and every spiritual leader on your planet speak of Ying and Yang.

You can not know joy without knowing pain. You can not know light without knowing darkness. How would You tell the difference? Both must exist. And I tell You, You can not know life without knowing death.

These are just the truths of the universe, my truths. I want you to fully understand and experience all that there is. You can not know LOVE unless you know hate. You can not know peace unless you know unrest.

You are learning from everything. You are experiencing all things as I have meant for You to, the highs and the lows. The highs are much higher after the lows, just as the water is much more quenching after the thirst. That is how You truly come to appreciate what You have been given.

Yet as it is, You still take everything I give You for granted. You take your eyesight for granted, You take each other for granted, You take your planet for granted. Did I teach You such ungratefulness? Did I teach You to abandon each other on this planet and fend for Yourselves?

Your Indians did not. Why do You? Ask any nation that has ever achieved peaceful communal harmony if they believe there is no God. It is those of You who are unharmonious that claim no God, looking for a scape goat to blame rather than blame Yourselves. You are avoiding personal responsibility.

Is it God's fault that there is hunger and war? Is it God's fault people act in hate and not in peace? How long will You be a group of people who take no responsibility for what you create and how your actions affect each other or their planet. Will You stand as part of that group or not?

One day regardless, You will come to Me either as a whole being or on bended knee with a broken spirit and ask Me to help You. And I will lovingly hold out my hand and say... this way my child. I have been here all along."

PART ONE

MY DIALOGUE WITH God
Contrary Action

Chapter 4
-    Just A Miracle

"Deus can planto vos quisquam vos volo futurus, tamen vos have ut loco panton in suus manuum."

"God can make you anything you want to be, but you have to put everything in his hands."

Mahalia Jackson

I was told all my life that I needed to listen more. As a child I talked a lot in school and it was always mentioned on my report card "talks too much in class." A few years ago I was told by at least three different people within one week that I had a problem listening. My current boyfriend said I always interrupted him and didn't listen. My boss said I never listen to how he wants things done, and that I won't take his direction. One of my girlfriends told me I don't listen to her feelings. She said: "Wendy you just talk right through my feelings, telling me I shouldn't feel this way and shouldn't feel that way, but you don't listen to me." I had been told this for years by my teachers, my parents, etc. But I didn't listen. Go figure.

Now however, I was able to listen to all of them for some reason. Since I had been hearing God, lots of things had been changing in my life. I had become very willing to look at myself honestly and I sincerely wanted to change this about myself, if it were true. One day I was walking through a book store thinking about what my friends had said. I thought to myself that I wanted to know the truth. I wanted God to give me a sign: "Am I Listening?" Right then and there I had a feeling to stop in my tracks and look to my right. There on the shelf next to me was a row of books with their bindings lined up facing me. All except for one. There was one single book sticking out of the row with it's cover page facing me directly. It was called "Are You Listening?"by Gloria Copeland in big bold letters. Of course the book was about learning to listen. I had to laugh because God is so funny.

But I tell you that story because God answers. He really does. If we are listening we will hear him. We have to look for the signs and wonders. There were hundreds of books in that store and on that shelf. They could have been about any other subject, yet the only one facing me was "Are You Listening?" I broke into tears and from that moment on I made every effort to listen like I had never listened before. My life and relationships have changed tremendously since I started to listen: to employers, friends, family, people's opinions, ideas, etc. Even if I don't agree with them, I listen. (Although sometimes I forget to and I have to remind myself.)

Anyway, that is how God works. He hears your plea and somehow gets the material world to cooperate in delivering you information. Don't ask me how, I don't know, and frankly I don't need to know. I put that in the category of "things I will never understand nor be able to explain." Like Love. It exists but it can't be explained, not really. We don't know why we feel it or how long it will last, or even where it comes from. We can't put Love on a table for all to see and describe it. You try! Describe Love. Think of someone you love, now take that feeling and set it on the desk in front of you and describe it. Where does it come from? What does it look like? How much does it weigh? What color or shape is it? Explain it to me. Prove to me that you Love them.

You can't prove LOVE physically but you know in your heart and are convinced that Loves exists, right? And so it is with God. We can't "prove" God exists or explain how He works, anymore than we can "prove" the existence of Love. We can describe the feelings of Love. We can point to the evidence of love: people living together, taking care of each other, and risking their lives for each other.

We can describe the feelings of God or talk about the "coincidences" that happen, but we can't point God out in a crowd and describe what He looks like or what He's wearing. We can't give Him a definite shape, or color, or tell how much He weighs. We can't put God on a table and have scientists analyze Him. We don't know where He came from, or why, or how He exists...but we can feel Him with our heart.

And when we close our eyes and pray, a sense of peace comes over us, we feel the warmth, the gentleness within, that takes place. When we pray to God in a crisis for his help and all of a sudden calmness comes over us, we can feel God. We don't how God works. He just does. I gave up having to have the answers or facts about God a long time ago. I don't need facts in order to rely on HIM. I don't think he can ever be explained.

And what difference does it make anyway? We all have so many explanations in our various religions of what we "think" God is. The world is fighting over these explanation as we speak. And yet none of them can be taken as "fact." God is unexplainable, just like love. So I simply put Him in the category of the unexplainable and I am certainly not going to argue with somebody about Him. Not even my Minister who I love and respect.

We can see the results of Love. And we can see the results of God. Whenpeople rely on this unexplainable God, their lives change, they become calmer, more productive. They become more loving and more purposeful people. When they pray to this unexplainable God and become aligned with God's energy we can see the peace in their face and we can tell by the kindness of their actions that they are with God.

And yet, we have no more proof than before. No, we can't prove LOVE or God visually, they can only be felt with the heart. Why isn't that proof enough? Science says visual proof is the least conclusive. Helen Keller said "the best and most beautiful things in the world can not be seen or even touched - they must be felt with the heart."

God is an energy like Love, invisible, yet powerfully present. Perhaps He IS the energy of LOVE. The Bible says God is Love. Some of the reoccurring questions across the planet are: Are we alone in this universe? Who is God and Why am I here? Don't you think it's strange that since the beginnings of mankind, they have always asked the question...Who is God?

The indication seems to be that somewhere inside ourselves we all have a knowing of God, a feeling of God in our hearts. People from all over the world, from different countries, cultures, centuries, and languages, without even speaking to each other, have developed thousands of religions trying to explain our magnificent invisible God. Societies are based on our beliefs and explanations about God. Ninety-five% of the planet believes in God. There is an inner intuition, a connection to God, that we all have and if we get on our knees and ask this energy to fill us, guide us, show us the way, He answers. When we get in alignment with God's energy or God's Loving energy...life goes well for us. People have testified to that all over the world. People's lives change and Love within them expands.

However, when we get out of alignment with the loving energy that is God we get into war, hatred, racism, sexism. The proof of God exists in the demonstration of our behavior. When God is present deeply within a person the rest of the world bows down in humility and an overwhelming sense of awe fills you. A feeling comes over you that cannot be explained but you know it in your soul.

Think how you feel about Jesus, Mother Theresa, Nelson Mandela, Buddah, Ghandi and Martin Luther King. In the presence of those people you feel the truth in the deepest part of your heart. You know God is with them. When God speaks loudly through people they have great impact. When a person omits God from their being the impact is also powerful as with Hitler or Stalin. The presence or absence of God is the most powerful factor in a human life. It's the whole enchilada.

Each moment we can choose to open ourselves up to the loving energy of God by consciously choosing it. That is our daily task...to choose God, to consciously choose Love in all situations. This book is not about being a God freak or a religious fanatic. This book is about spirituality and your true purpose here. We are all spiritual beings here to discover ourselves through our relationship with the source of spirit. This book is about a Trinity: Your relationship with God, Your relationship to yourself, and Your relationship with others.

Like the Christian trinity of the Father, Son and the Holy Ghost, all three parts are individual expressions of the same entity: God. So is the Trinity between Yourself, God and Others. All three elements are God. You are God expressing Himself, other people are God expressing Himself. God is all there is. Your relationship with God is all that matters. Your relationship to God, Yourself and Others is all that matters. The 10 commandments are all about relationships, nothing else

The relationship with God is a necessary part of our true spirituality regardless of what religion we are or ideas we may have about life. Our relationship with God is the relationship with our true spiritual self. You can try to deny it, but deep in your heart you know there is a source to your spirit, and in your darkest hour you always call God, your father, to help you because you know that is your source and your only salvation, a place of miracles and a place of real power. Remember him in all moments not only when your soul cries out in your darkest despair but also in your greatest victories.

Does God exist? To complete this discussion I will simply will share something my friend Lee said to me one day said "Wendy, if I go though my life acting like there is no God and get to the end of my life and find out that there is a God, I am screwed. So I am going to live my life like there IS a God, and if at the end I find out there isn't, oh well I won't lose a thing. But if I find out there is... I am a winner. I win either way."

I sing a song on my CD As I Am called "Just A Miracle," that was written by my good friend Stephen Cahill, film and television composer for the series, "Touched by An Angel." This song perfectly describes the miracle I have experienced by developing my relationship with God.

JUST A MIRACLE

The moment that I met you
Amazing how I knew
That you'd become a part of me
And I a part of you
The minute that I held you
You reached me deep inside
I knew I'd never be the same
My world had opened wide
And how did this
Come to be?
I am You and You are me
And though I've searched high and low
There's only one good reason that I know
It's just a miracle
I'm gonna love you all my days
It's just a miracle
It's like a dream a yet it stays
And all the trouble past now at last
There's only joy to find
Love is life's miracle... and You are mine.

You can buy my CD "As I Am" at www.CDbaby.com

PART ONE

MY DIALOGUE WITH God

Contrary Action

Chapter 5
-   God is Within

*"Sulum alio est a Deus in complexo.
Suus tantum votum est nascor."*

*"Every person is a God in embryo. Its
only desire is to be born"*

Deepak Chopra

Everyday I start my day by saying "God's Will Be Done, Not mine. I ask for His guidance for my day and ask that I be who He would have me be in every circumstance with every person I come in contact with. This prayer elevates me to a higher level of being and the days I forget to say this are never as good as the days I remember. Of course I can always say it as soon as I remember.

Getting into alignment with God's Will for my life. This was a confusing concept to me in the beginning, because I didn't know what God's Will was. Which of the many religions were right about God's Will? There is so much conflict in the world about who is "right" about God. I stay out of those discussions. I have come to realize through my writing and my many dialogues with God that His Will is and always will be LOVE. His Will is not some theological concept that you'll never be able to understand. It is very simple: Always come from Love, towards yourself and towards others. If it isn't Loving, don't do it. His Will is always about taking the higher road. He has told me His Will is always about thinking of yourself less often and more often about other people. His Will is always about giving, being of service, compromising, following your hearts dream's and desires, trusting yourself, loving yourself, and knowing you are one with God.

His Will is for us to remember our own greatness, that He is within us, and where he is - is Holy Ground. You are Holy Ground. Don't ever treat yourself or others less than that. His Will is also for you to remember God is in every one and where they stand is Holy Ground. Treat them as such. There is no need to fight, no need to war, if we believe these truths. The pain and suffering in the world comes from people not believing this. Rather they believe they are less than God. They believe God is somewhere other than within us all. If we all could recognize that in each face we see God we would treat each other with Love and respect. Most of the worlds problems can be traced to not seeing God within each other or seeing God within ourseleves.

For getting in touch with the truth of who you are and aligning yourself with God can only be done by going within yourself and getting silent. To know His Will you must go within and pray that He puts you in the best possible position to understand His Will for you. The answers cannot be found in books, religions or other people's explanations of God's Will. Even this book is not a replacement for the work you must do by yourself in silent meditation with God. I can tell you that it's all about Love. But only

God can really point you in that direction. You have read many books about this. You have heard that Love is the answer. This isn't new information. One more book isn't going to make the difference. Only a direct, personal relationship with Him will enable the Divine Intervention you need to send your life in a brand new direction. You can keep trying to find the answer outside of you, but has this worked for you so far?

People struggle in life because they think the answers to life lie outside of themselves. They think they need the house, the car, the validation and approval of others, the toys, money, friendships, wealth, power, prestige and property. Yet all these things, however nice, are just diversions. All that external seeking is not really about the houses, the cars, or any of that stuff- it's about feelings of self worth. It's about believing that if we have and do all of these things then we will finally be worthy of Loving ourselves and being Loved by others. But if you knew God was within you and that you are Holy right now, you would know that you are already worthy. If everyone knew the truth about themselves and each other we would all feel worthy right now. But most of us don't get it. Somehow we still think so little of ourselves. We underestimate God.

I think most people realize that God exists and even believe He is the answer during the dark moments of their lives, when the path is arduous or the loss is great. For a split second we return to God and know the answer is with Him. As life returns to normal, we return to our normal search of looking for fulfillment outside of ourselves. Even though deep down in our hearts we know we felt God and we felt the answer for that brief moment. We felt the comfort and Love of God and then walked away once we felt a little bit better. That's what most people do.

We use our senses to define our lives. We eat a ripe orange and the juice tastes delicious on our tongues. We feel the warmth of a fire on our skin. We smell the heavenly aroma of a pie baking in the oven. We touch our children or Lover, and can feel the closeness. Our senses give reality to our experiences. The problem howver with seeing that God is within is that our eyes can't look inside of the body and see God the same way they can see a mountain or sunset with all its magnificent colors.

When we cut open the human body we can't find God. Where is he, in the arm? When we cut open the body where is the soul? We can't point it out and identify it. Therefore, since we can't prove God physically, we doubt Him. This mental barrier supports the idea that God must be outside of us or that the answer lies elsewhere. So it is only with the eyes of the heart that we can look in and see God and reconnect to the Love of God within us.

Many of us know of God, but if we are ever to know God we must practice the discipline of going within through prayer and meditation. We must learn to sit quietly in the silence where God resides. It is only in this beautiful silence that we can hear God.

We may not be able to prove that he is physically within us but when we meditate we can feel that he is within our hearts. In the same way that the eyes of the heart see the heart of another person when we're "in Love." We can't explain why we feel "in Love" but the feeling is real. We can't show you the "in Love" feeling in a material way, but we can feel it. We know it is real and that it's one of the most powerful experiences on earth. It makes us lose all sense of self for a moment while we're lost in rapture. Temporarily, colors seem brighter. Llife seems more exciting and everything seems right in the world. We can't prove Love physically anymore than we can prove God physically but somehow we know they both exist.

Meditation is a discipline that pays off after you have practiced it. It is a spiritual awakening takes place over time. People often have short spiritual experiences which convince them of God's presence temporarily. It awakens their awareness of God. They suddenly feel God, know they are not alone, and that there is something greater than them. But once that brief experience is over, most people seem to lose their awareness of once again.

In order to retain that awareness you must practice the discipline of consistent, silent meditation. You must take the action of meditation first to reap the rewards of the results later. It is the same thing with courage. Courage doesn't come until you do the thing you fear. You develop courage after doing the thing you fear. Courage is a by-product of action. Reconnection to your soul, inner self, highest self, God, only comes after the actions of meditation and prayer. As with most things, you can't put the cart before the horse.

To change your life and learn to Love yourself and others, you must utilize the tool of Meditation. Not only will it help you develop a conscious contact with God but also the characteristics of Love. When you Meditate you can start hearing God's Will for you. Remember God is LOVE. God's Will is always others-centered. Our Will is always self-centered. You cannot serve God and your selfishness at the same time. The correct use of your own personal will power is to use it to do God's Will. You must learn to suppress instant gratification or self-will and serve a higher will other than your own, Love.

It will take sacrifice and forcing yourself to meditate when you really don't want to. Many people have a hard time quieting their mind, so sitting in silent Meditation will not be easy for many people. But with practice it becomes easier ans easier and soon becomes comfortable. Meditation will help you get to that inner peace and communication with God that you so desperately seek. Through Meditation, communion with God is possible at anytime.

Meditation and also prayer is the answer to peacefulness within, to a sense of connectedness to God and the way to experience the Love energy that God is and that is already within us. That Love is the key to health and energy. That Love is the key to balance and harmony. When you get quiet and go within yourself you can hear your heart beating and your breathing. These are sounds you don't usually hear throughout the course of your busy day of phones ringing, traffic, conversations, etc. Your heart is always beating but only in silence can you hear it. It is the same with the voice of God. He is always there but you can hear Him best in the silence.

Meditation will help you to hear God and be guided by His Love when you feel like hating. You'll forgive when you feel like punishing. You'll be kind when you feel like saying hurtful things. Once you are able to do that you will have developed the heart and character of some of God's most precious creations: Jesus, Martin Luther King, Mother Theresa, Mahatma Ghandi, etc. All of these people sacrificed themselves for others. Love is about sacrificing yourself for others. To be like these people you must develop the spiritual muscles of the discipline to meditate, sacrifice, surrender and align your thoughts, words, and actions with God's Will. Meditation is how we learn that God is within and can discover God's Will for ourselves.

Of course Monks mediate and other highly spiritual people. But how are we normal folk going to implement the practice of meditation into our daily lives? How much time are we going to spend with God? We work. We pay rent, and let's face it most of us aren't going to an isolated location and sit under a tree for years like the Buddah. We have bills to pay, responsibilities to meet and movies to see! Yet we know something is missing from our daily lives, that we have a deeper purpose, a higher calling. We all do. In the face of our busy complicated liveswe must find a way to increase the amount of time we spend alone with God. We can all do that if we make the effort.

How does increasing our time with God affect the

rest of the world? The Bible says "The kingdom of heaven is within" so it stands to reason that if we want to have more peaceful lives we have to spend more time going within. The peace we gain from meditation will help us treat each other with more kindness and love. The closeness we feel to God and the Love we experience from being close to Him, will motivate us to do more for other people, helping others to improve their lives, which in turn imporves our own. .

But let's get specific. This book is about practical and powerful solutions. Ask yourself what can I do today? Can you start giving 10 or 15 minutes of your time per day to sit in stillness and quiet oneness with God?

We can work, play, have romance, raise our children and also meditate. As an American woman, in a country of great wealth and freedoms, one luxury we have is time. Weekends, evenings, vacations and many moments here and there.

If you looked back into your life and added up the hours of television you watched compared to the hours you communed with the God within you what would your results be? For me I can't even begin to count the hours of television I have watched in my life. It would be easier to count how rarely I have out all things aside and sat quietly by myself going within and being silent with God. That is where you find God...in the silence within yet we so rarely go to that place.

Mother Theresa said it simply in her book "In The Heart of The World,"

"Listen in silence because if your heart is full of other things you cannot hear the voice of God. But when you have listened to the voice of God in the stillness of your heart, then your heart is filled with God."

We don't have to strive for perfection. We don't have to compare ourselvs to masters of spirituality and spiritual discipline and always feel less than them. We don't have to be so hard on ourseleves. We only have to do one thing... increase the amount of time we spend in silent, still communion with God. That's all. The rest will take care of itself. The only thing you have to master is training yourself to meditate, disciplining yourself to sit in the stillness where you can find God as often as you can.

I don't have all the answers. I don't claim to be a spiritual guru. I hope I can help people in my lifetime find God. I know when I meditate for even 10 minutes in a day I feel more peaceful. I feel more connected to God and because I write what comes to me in meditation, I get answers to the questions I have. A few things that I know for sure are: If you ask... you will receive. This has happened to me so many times I can't even count them. If you ask for the truth of God He will show himself to you using the universe around you.

If you train yourself to sit in the stillness... you will run into God there. God is not elusive. He is ever present and waiting for you to come to Him. He is patient, He is permanent.

You suffer in your absence from him. He is not absent from you. The world suffers from their absence from Him. If this book tells you nothing, let it tell you this:

GO WITHIN and you will not GO WITHOUT.

God made it that easy for us. Easier than we ever could have dreamed possible. Why do we make it so difficult? Why do we cause ourselves and others so much pain? Stop the madness people! Relax, just sit still and get quiet. God is within the stillness of all of us

SO GO BE WITH HIM.

Contrary Actions:

1)   Learn How to Meditate. Get a how-to book today and begin to study the art.

2)   Join a Meditation class.

3)   Use guided Meditation tapes or CDs to help you get started Meditating. There are many available. I suggest Wayne Dyer's 'Into The Gap."

4)   Use guided Visualization tapes to help you begin the practice of using your imagination and mind to create a peaceful reality within. Then you can expand on your new ability to sit still and relax, and incorporate silent Mediation.

4)   Watch one less TV show per day. Go to one less ball game. Have one less argument with a Loved one. Instead, Meditate!

PART ONE

MY DIALOGUE WITH God
Contrary Action

Chapter 6
-   I Am Not Religious

"Permissum vestri monastica exsisto minor of a ratio quod magis of a diligo res."

"Let your religion be less of a theory and more of a love affair."

Gilbert K. Chesterton

Religion often obstructs the path to God. I am not religious. I am spiritual. People get so caught up in their "religions," they forget to practice the qualities of LOVE/God in their every day life; kindness, patience, and unconditional love. In our world right now we have Muslim extremists so fantatical about their "religion," that they are willing to kill over it. Is this killing a quality of a loving God? They actually have lost sight of the loving principles the Islam religion teaches. As explained in "The Way To Truth," Islam is epitomized in the most frequently recited of all Quranic phrases, the Basmala — In the name of God, the Merciful (al-Rahman), the Compassionate (al-Rahim). Both words are related to the quality of rahma, meaning mercy and compassion. God manifests Himself essentially through His absolute, all-inclusive Mercy and Compassion, and Islam is founded upon that affirmation. Islamic extremists have forgotten these principals.

The christian religion is a group with members who believe their religion is the only true religion and therefore, they spend much of their energy trying to force their ideas down people's throats insisting everyone else's religions or paths to God are invalid! Jehova's Witness are a prime example of this.

I actually was in a church the other day that was

talking about people bearing much "fruit," with fruit being good works. The pastor then unbelievably said "only Christians can bear fruit." In other words only Christians can do good deeds. I almost stood up and said outloud, "Are you kidding me? I bet there are people in this world that have done more good deeds than the "Christians" in this room!" I can't believe that Christians think their way is the only way to God. It is so arrogant.

And I guess we should just wipe out all of the good that has been done by people of every culture who are not Christians. Obviously "it doesn't count" anyway. Religion is a scary thing. It shouldn't be but it is. There are too many interpretations of holy writings around the world. People are flawed and have transferred these flawed characteristics to God. I think among the worst characteristics of human beings is their judgmentalism and intolerance of other peoples' differences and religions. Looking back through history at people like Ghengis Khan, Napolean, Stalin, Hitler, Burning of the Witches, Enslaving the Blacks, Yugoslavian ethnic cleansing and the way women are treated all through out the Middle East we can see the biggest atrocities are caused by judging others and being intolerant of eachother's differences.

Judging, hating, burning, cleansing, these are human qualities. NOT the qualities of God. Do you really believe that a loving God is made up of our worst human traits? That God is intolerant of other religions, races, colors, and paths to God? I find that hard to believe when I look around at the amazing diversity created by God in every facet of life, nature and human beings. It seems to me that God is a lover of diversity and variety. No, my God is bigger than the worst of people. So much biggerI believe each religion has many wonderful principles.

I am an eternal spiritual being having a spiritual experience. I am spiritual. To me, being Spiritual means I have a connection to my spirit and the spirit of God inside me - outside of organized religions that tries to intimiate every other religion. My relationship with God is based on a one to one relationship I have daveloped with Him as I speak to Him in my prayers and He answers me in my meditations. I ask him directly for His will for me and the power to carry it out.

I do attend various churches and study various religions because I appreciate the beauty of many paths to God. I love some of the rituals of Buddism, Catholicism and born again Christians. I usually go to a Presbytarian church. I love the Praise band and Worship in my church. I love the people singing to God with such passion and conviction. I call myself a Christian because I try to be like Christ. But I admire anyone's reverence and devotion to God, whatever their religion. We live in a world of millions of people. With different cultures, races, customs, religions and ways of honoring God. My minster may disagree, however, I do not believe any one group of people have exclusive rights on understanding God. Nor do I believe that God only talks to one particular group or another. I believe he talks with all of us, in many forms, in many different ways. I try to see God in all people, in all traditions and in all religions despite their differences.

"As long as people are fighting over whose God is the "right" God, people will never settle into peaceful observance of a loving God and be able to treat each other in a Loving Way. Human beings are not here to argue about who has the right interprtation of God that misses the point. We are here to evolve from being driven by EGO to being driven by God and Love; to be used in service to others. Each person's life is that journey. And we can either use the experiences we go through to become closer to Love or we can drift further from it. We can all use the experiences that happen to us to decide who we are going to be in relation to the things that happen to us. I choose to act from love in relation to all things that happen to me. This is my choice. It isn't always easy and it doesn't mean I have it down pat yet. I don't.

When we learn from our mistakes we often learn valuable lessons. If we don't learn from them we are likely to repeat them. Experiences give us the opportunity to learn to have a loving response to all situations. Some people go through life believing the experiences that happen to them are random and have no significant spiritual meaning. However, they do have meaning. The purpose of life is to become a being that eminates love at all times. This is a life long process and journey and all things that happen to you, everyone you meet, every disappointment and every success is made specifically for you to choose to react in love to that experience. Your life is not random and neither are the things that happen in it.

Life is like a Spectrum. On one end of the Spectrum you have God or LOVE. On the other end of the Spectrum is the EGO. The EGO's most salient characteristic is Fear.

To me God and Love are the same thing. You may call your understanding of God; the Universe, Great Spirit in the Sky, Mother Nature, Christ, Almighty, Lord, Jehovah or Holy Sprit. To Hindus He is Adi Purush, Akal Purakh to the Sikhs, Yahweh to Jews, Allah to Muslims, and more than 25 names to the Africans, etc. Whatever you call God it really doesn't matter.

What matters is that there are two voices within you. One voice connected to God or your Highest Self, and the other is connected to your Ego or Your Lowest Self. The highest part of who we are is in fact the essence of God dwelling within us. As blood runs through our veins, God runs through our soul. The voice of our highest self is always guiding us towards the Love end of the Spectrum. The voice of the EGO is always pulling us the other way. That is the battle of good and evil, which exists within each one of us.

Fear is always the absence of Love. The loving thing to do is always to be forgiving, compassionate, tolerant and kind. The fearful thing is always selfish, vengeful, punishing, defensive, inconsiderate and self-centered. The EGO is always self-centered. A person cannot be self-centered and God-centered at the same time. It is one or the other.

People's actions and reactions are not really personal to you, they simply signify where they fall on the Spectrum. These are based solely on past experiences and the choices people are making now about acting from Love or Fear. It has nothing to do with you. Although people's reactions to you seem very personal, they really are not.

How we treat people, even those who have hurt us determines where we fall on the Spectrum. Always remember that regardless of what others do to us, we are all measured spiritually by OUR place on the Spectrum.

The battle between good and evil goes on internally and the universe sets up perfect scenarios to test you and help you make choices about where you are going to fall on the Spectrum. People push your buttons, laws are unfair, your children misbehave, your boss wrongly fires you, people cheat on you in relationships, someone cuts you off, the line is too long at the grocery store, someone talks badly about you, a friend betrays you, etc. How do we choose to react to these events? It all depends on where you fall on the Spectrum

When people say or do mean things to you, what is your reaction? Do you take it personally and come from EGO by retaliating, attacking them verbally, physically or even passively by ignoring them? Or do you take the high road, come from Love, and offer forgiveness, patience and compassion remembering that people are human and not perfect. God gives us the power to choose our reactions. He wants us to make these choices so we can choose to come from Love. In choosing Love we are deciding who we are going to be. It is not dictated to us. Deciding is very powerful.

Every situation that happens to you is an opportunity to decide to move closer to God/Love or to move further away.

Each person's life is a journey to God. The Universe offers us the same experiences over and over with different people and slightly different scenarios that give us opportunities to make different choices. Often people believe these experiences are random and have no significant spiritual meaning, but I tell you that is not the case. They are on purpose to give us an opportunity to know God. We will recreate and relive what we need to learn until we learn it and move closer to God. Then we will have new experiences where we can learn to undo something else inside of us which stands in the way of our relationship to God.

There is one layer after another of fear that stands in the way of loving ourselves, other people and even God. Our job is to peel away these layers, like the layers of an onion until we get to the inner core where only God resides. That means we have to shed our fear, our pride, our EGO, our need to be right, to prove others wrong, to hurt, to defend, to retaliate, to pay back, to lie, to steal, to avoid, abuse, misuse etc. Instead, we must act from Love no matter what happens. This will be very hard sometimes, especially when people are acting unloving towards us. It's easy to Love nice people. It's the not-so-nice people that are hard to love. But those are the challenges we are here to overcome.

Some people we know of are or have become aware that this is how life works, people like Depak Chopra, Marianne Williamson, Gary Zukav, and Neale Donald Walsh. Enlightened people use every single experience on earth to measure how THEY themselves are doing on the Spectrum. Because ultimately that's all that will really come into play if there is a God who judges our life here when we get to the end and it's time to transition.

When "enlightened" people see they are not being loving, they alter THEIR actions or reactions to be more like God/LOVE-like. "Enlightened" simply means they have made conscious choices that have moved them closer to the light or God-Love end of the Spectrum. People who master this become heralded by the world and revered because they have brought their actions into alignment with the true nature of their Spirit and with God. Examples of these people are Jesus, Mahatma Ghandi, Rev. Martin Luther King, Mother Theresa, Buddah or any of the other great teachers. These people touch us deeply inside because we know they have achieved an extraordinary level of spiritual enlightenment. However, we wonder how they got there. We assume they must be different than us, better somehow, but they are not. We are all made equally with the same seed of Love within us. The only difference between Mother Theresa and you is choices. What are you committed to? They got there by choice. They chose peace instead of war, Love instead of fear, God instead of EGO. Enlightened people use every single experience to measure how THEY themselves are doing on the Spectrum. Because ultimately that's all that counts.

When people don't use life's experiences in this way, they simply go through life as victims blaming others for what happens to them. They are angry, bitter, resentful, greedy, prideful, hurtful, and entirely unhappy within. They are searching for meaning in external things and believe that if only they have the right car, a big house, money, the right job, fame, power, and on and on, that THEN they are finally going to be happy so and be their "true" self.

However, just ask those who have attained all the material possessions that are "supposed" to make you happy and see if they are truly happy. Better yet, consider this statistic. The highest suicide rate in California is in Beverly Hills. Inner happiness is only found when you are living on the Love-God end of your Spiritual Spectrum. To achieve that, one must begin to recognize this amazing life for what it really is: a training ground, with various exercises (Experiences) to develop your spiritual muscle. "God" muscles if you will."

Even people fighting over whose God is the "right" God, and whose beliefs are the "right beliefs" are acting from somewhere on the Spectrum. Many of these people are closer to the Fear-EGO end than they think they are. But don't tell them that, they will kill you... in the name of God! As long as people have to be right about their ideas and beliefs and continue to make others wrong for their beliefs, people will never settle into a peaceful, loving observance of each other and God. Until we all learn to come from Love we will not be able to tolerate one another's differences and be able to treat each other in a loving way. To learn to come from Love we must simply ask the question: What Would Love Do?

People in the world could do more to take care of everyone else in it, but too many people have not gotten "right" with God yet. By that I mean they have not connected to their own Soul in a way that has freed them from greed, EGO, need of power, need to dominate, possess, control and abuse others. They are not coming strictly from Love.

You are in charge of what you bring into your world and into the world of those around you. We each get to make a wonderful choice every moment of everyday. Who are we going to be in relation to what is happening to us? We can change our minds at anytime. What we did in the last moment doesn't bind us to that choice for all future moments, because we have free will. That is what that means. Each moment we are free to make a new choice. If we don't like how we have reacted to someone we can change it. If we don't like the way we are treating ourselves we can change it. If we don't like the kind of relationships we are in we can change them. If we don't like our job, the kind of parent we are being etc., ad finitum, we can change it simply with our conscious choice to do so.

I love life, I love the opportunity life affords us to learn how to do this. I love becoming a better person each day. A kinder, more considerate, nicer person. One who thinks well of herself and yet thinks of herself less often. A person who goes out of her way to help other people and really wants to make a helpful contribution to the world.

There is a little saying by Linda Ellis about what's written on tombstones, the beginning year, the ending year and the dash right in the middle that goes like this;

"What are you going to do with your dash? For the

dash represents all the time that you spend on earth. And only those who love you know what that little line is worth. For it matters not, how much we own, the cars, the house, the cash. What matters is how we live and love, and how we spend our dash."

Wow. During my dash, I am trying to become the fullest expression of who I am, not to be governed by fear in anyway. I am working hard to share my gifts and talents with the world and most importantly, being kind to others no matter what they do or say, simply because I want to be a kind and loving person. My mentors are Christ, Ghandi, and the Buddah and I have some deep foot steps to follow in. Here is my personal concept of God, as I understand God.

Here is my personal concept of God, as I understand God.

God is the Energy that is at the root of all things. The force that programs the flower to bloom, the life energy and force within the seed. God is the force of nature working together in perfect harmony, balance and communication. God is always supporting every creature towards the fullfillment of it's potential. God is the all knowing, knower of the universe, invisible as the wind.

God is the Energy that is at the root of all things. The force that programs the flower to bloom, the life energy and force within the seed. God is the force of nature working together in perfect harmony, balance and communication. God is always supporting every creature towards the fullfillment of it's potential. God is the all knowing, knower of the universe, invisible as the wind.

God is the most powerful force in life. Perfect order. Perfect Structure. Perfect Planning. God is intention. The one who has created perfect reason, perfect lessons, the perfect fitting together of all things. Existence is a perfectly oiled machine thanks to God. God creates, and has created us as co-creative beings with itself. My God supports my growth. My God has created a Divine seed in me and intends for it to bloom into a perfect Rose. My God is in that seed and in that Rose. My God is the force behind me and within me - and orchestrates all of nature and life to support the flowering of my Rose.

My God is loving. Patient. Supportive. Reliable. Unwaivering. The same allthrough time. Never changing. My God has always existed. My God is everywhere at the same time. My God loves me. Without judgement. My God is Love.

What is YOUR personal concept of God?

PART ONE

MY DIALOGUE WITH God

Contrary Action

Chapter 7
-    What God said to Me

"Exsisto curiosus quisnam vos subpono foedus per. Illic es qui per consanguinei per lemma mos plumbum vos propinquus ut Mihi , quod qui mos plumbum vos porro me."

"Be careful who you forge alliances with. There are those who by relation with them will lead you closer to Me, and those who will lead you further from Me."

God

When we underestimate or judge what God has created or is providing for us we get into trouble. Can't God determine what is best for us? Why do we keep trying to second-guess God? Why don't we accept things as they are and accept that God loves us and knows what he is doing.

We get into trouble when we are trying to hold on to things because we are familiar with them even when they are not good for us. We get into trouble when we continue to be angry at people for things they do when we don't understand what lessons they may be teaching us. You cannot control the outcome of your life or certain experiences. Only God can do that. Missing a crack in the sidewalk, not walking under ladders. Do you think these silly ideas are more powerful than God? Do you think they impact His master plan for you?

God's will is mighty and ever powerful. Eventually you will do God's Will because when you don't the Universe will set you back with an unexpected dose of reality that always leads you right back where you started from: At the crossroads between your will and God's Will. Life will teach you the same lessons over and over until you are finally willing to surrender and follow God's Will.

We cannot know what God has intended for us. We

cannot know what the highest outcome is. But be assured God only has the highest outcome intended for us. The pain may confuse you but the pain is only there to get your attention.

Therefore trust in God. Accept that things in your life have and are happening for a reason as God has intended, and when you don't understand what God is doing ASK HIM and ye shall receive.

In case you were wondering, He is not here to let us down. He exists to celebrate and exhault us as we are here to celebrate and exhault Him and all of life. His working unfolds in the most complicated and simple ways. They are truly magical. He is a Genius, an Artist, a Master Creator.

Know Him and Ye shall know yourself, for you are created in His likeness and image. You are the greatest being He has ever created, therefore do not judge yourself as less than magnificent, because you simply are magnificence in every sense of the word. A perfect being created in the image of God. Think nothing else of yourself for it would simply be untrue. God has created a masterpiece and that masterpiece is You.

WHAT GOD WANTS ME TO TELL YOU:

It's okay to let go. I will catch you when you fall.

You feel like you're giving up more than you really are.

But that is all an illusion You are releasing what is not best for you.

You are releasing a poison that has infested you and I will draw it out-.

Let me show you where you need to go and where you need to be.

Follow me for I am your true leader and I will not steer you wrong.

Take a breath, hold my hand and let me lead you to the light of God.

This pain and suffering you have imposed on you self is nothing compared to the pain and suffering you will feel if you keep trying to do your will. I have told you over and over .

Hear my voice. Let no one steer you from me or from the Kindgom of Heaven.

Let no human have power over you especially one who has power to take you in a direction that is not leading to me

I have told you loud and clear who you need to follow
the rest is up to you. I have all the faith in you in the
world and I know you will do what is right for you
and what I want for you.

Hold on be strong and let me lead you. Release all
that is not of me, all that is not of God.

You belong to no one but God.

You are His, He is yours.

You cannot belong to other people.

You can experience them.

Share Ideas with them, laugh with them, feel pain,
tears and joy with them

but you do not belong to them

and they do not belong to you.

All of my children belong to me.

It is only a matter of whether they claim their own
birth right.

I have given you the Kingdom of Heaven and I have
plans and ideas for each and every one of you.

Therefore, let not the ideas of others have more
sinificance or power over you or your direction than
Mine.

That is what happens when we falsely believe we
belong to other people.

*We feel responsible for following their ideas and
their paths or their needs
You do not have the authority to act in such a maner.
I have instructed you clearly that I am your path
I am your salvation, I am your life and any other
choice will lead you into a world of pain away from
your truest purpose:
Communion With God.
Therefore, be careful who you forge alliances with.
There are those who by relation with them
will lead you closer to Me
and those who will lead you further from Me.
but always remember you belong to none of them,
You only belong to Me.
I Am your savior, I Am your teacher.
I Am your inspiration. I am the source of your being.
I Am the master of all creation
and you are My magnificent creations,
designed to live the life of God, as I see it.
One filled with Joy, Health, Peace, Abundance,
Prosperity and Love.
I Am not an egotist, I am not a hero.
I Am not a traitor or a dictator, I am not your enemy.
I Am the one who loves you,*

the Only one who truly loves you as you are meant
to be loved,
Mind, Body and Soul.
That is why you never feel completely full
by human Love.
It is through My Love that you will know Love.
It is through My Love that you will know yourself.
It is through My Love that you will be able to truly
Love Yourself.
It is only through My Love that you will truly be able
to Love Others.

You are creations of God, put here on this planet
to Give Love,
Receive Love,
and Be Love.

For I Am LOVE.

PART ONE

MY DIALOGUE WITH God

Contrary Action

Chapter 8
- My Dialogue With God

"Nos es Divinus satis sciscitor quod nos es maximus satis ut suscipio."

"We are Divine enough to ask and we are important enough to receive.."

Wayne Dyer

The following pages are dialogues or messages I received into my awareness directly after praying. I wrote them down, almost unable to keep up with them as they came. It is my belief that God was "speaking" to me and I was transcribing what he said.

Why are we here? Why do we exist? What is our purpose? These are some of the oldest questions known to human kind. Entire religions have been formed around the varying answers to these questions. (I don't need a Religion formed around these answers.) Since I was having this ongoing dialogue with God for several years now I decided one day that I really wanted to know the answers to the big questions.

So, I sat quietly in meditation and deep in my heart I asked him for the truth. As I did, I started getting that familiar feeling again that I needed to write. By now I was used to this miracle! It was almost like talking to a neighbor (sort of). I grabbed a piece of paper and took dictation, no editing.

If you ever wanted the finite answers about WHY WE ARE HERE, here they are. You can Meditate one every day

WHAT GOD WANTS ME TO TELL YOU:

We are here to Love.

We are here to experience Love in it's purest form.

We are here to Love ourselves.

We are here to Love God.

We are here to Love all there is.

We are here to express our souls deepest purpose.

We are here to follow our 1st creative ideas and make them manifest.

We are here to choose Love not fear.

We are here to not follow fear, doubt and others negativity and ideas.

We are here to choose Love in the presence of fear

We are here to choose faith in the presence of doubt.

We are here to choose peace in the presence of hate and war.

We are here to let go of external beliefs that don't support our highest purpose of our souls identity.

We are here to follow our highest thoughts and ideas.

We are here to follow our creative ideas.

We are here to experience joy, fulfillment, peace, health, harmony and Love.

We are here to know ourselves as God.

We are here to work as masters in understanding
and harmony with the laws of the universe.

We are here to accept and experience abundance.

We are here to accept and to know Love on every
level.

We are here to experience a state of joy and calm
in the face of all else.

We are here to give Love and to receive it.

We are here to let go of limited thoughts.

We are here to let go of limited definitions of our
true identity.We are here to be limitless.

We are here to be powerful creations of our
highest ideals.

We are here to be powerful creators.

We are here to be powerful healers.

We are here to be clear and free channels of
Love energy.

We are here to be embodied by the Love energy.

We are here to experience wonder and amazement,
gratitude and joy.

We are here to be thankful and honor the human
experience for it is our master teacher.

We are here to be amazed by life for it is

the magnificent expression of the soul's journey t

hrough it's experience back to God.

We are here to be amazed by the journey,

excited by the journey and not in fear of the journey.

There is no purpose other than to find God.

There is no purpose other than to honor God

There is no purpose other than to be of God mind,

soul and body.

There is no purpose higher or greater than God.

There is no reason to do things that are not of God's

highest will for us.

There is no reason to speak unless it is God's words.

There is no reason to play unless it is God's play.

There is no reason to be confused.

We are God. God is we. I am AM that I AM. I am God

There is no reason to be unless you are being of God.

There is no reason to touch unless it is with God's

hand There is no reason to breathe unless it is with

God's breath.

There is no reason to see unless it is with God's eyes.

There is no reason to feel unless it is with God's heart.

There is no reason to do anything but Love with

God's Love.

There is no reason to be anything other than

God's Love. God is all that we will ever need.

PART ONE

MY DIALOGUE WITH God
Contrary Action

Chapter 9
- Why Do We Feel So Empty?

"Solus via ut Deus est praecessi intus. Si nos operor non vado intus nos mos vado vacuus

The only way to God is to go Within. If we do not go within, we will go without.

Mother Theresa

We are all silently lashing out, consistently longing for more than we have. Why is it that what we have is never enough? One more car, one more friend, one more lover. Is the hole within us so deep it can never be filled? What put this "well" there? Was it God or was it ourselves and our underestimation of our worth? Was it the mistreatment by others or the mistreatment of ourselves that has made us feel so empty? Did we take a hurt so personally that we allowed it to expand our well? Do we want to spend our entire life trying to fill up a well that does not really exist? A well that God never put there, that was created by our own imagination and our overly misguided EGOs. It's incredible to think that God created the heavens and the earth and could not create human beings complete and whole.

It's incredible to think God would create humans with big gaping holes inside of them, never satisfied, always in pain, never Loved. For that would simply imply that we have a God who is unloving. No, we have a loving God. God created us whole. During one of my meditations God said to me: "We are to let go of the appearance of emptiness. You are not empty, let go of the appearance of emptiness. Let go of loneliness and separation, You are not alone. Let go of the need to be filled by others,

You are already filled by God, Yourself and the sheer nature of your creation"-God created you whole.

You need not want for anything, lack for nothing. You have nothing to fix, You are whole and full in God. Right here, right now where You are. You are whole. You need only to recognize and embrace that truth.

Happiness is right here for you. Lack is an appearance. You live in an abundant world, where there is more than enough of everything to go around. You have all that You need in this very moment. You are living in the Kindgom of Heaven as we speak and You only need ask God to help you recognize it.

But know this, your feelings of separation are only an illusion. The reason you feel empty is because you have the limited thought that attachment can only be physical or visual. By example, your hand is attached to your arm, your arm is attached to your body and that is the only way you are able to define attachment.

You underestimate God and the many ways you are truly attached to God. Is not our solar system attached to the universe? Are not water and air attached to your very existence? Separate entities, yet completely connected. Without one there is not the other. There are various levels of attachment.

Your attachment with God is a consistent undercurrent in your life. Constant and ever present, you feel God in a sudden burst of joy or a quiet moment of peace. We feel God in our darkest hour and often in the environment around us as a sun sets, flowers open, or a new baby is born. God is forever present. We must learn to rely on Him. You too can choose to experience God at any time by turning your attention on God and standing in God.

Often you may feel lost and separated from the great peace you know you are supposed to be experiencing. You feel disconnected from a place inside you that should be feeling content and joyous. That is because you have cut yourself off from the awareness of God.

You were not cut off from God as an infant. You were so close to God right after you were born. Your heart was open, your eyes were shining with light and everything you saw you looked upon with wonder and amazement. As you became aware of yourself and discovered your relation to your parents, to other people and to the earth, you determined yourself separate from all of these things. Likewise you determined yourself separate from God by saying I am not God so I must be other than God.

You also said if God is magnificent I certainly must be less than that.. After all He is God and I am just a person. This is the greatest of all LIES – You and God are One, completely attached. God is Within you. You can no more detach from Him than we can live without a heart. This misunderstanding is the root of all problems. Every human being is connected to and a part of God always.

However, because you "feel" you are separate and less than God you are often in fear. You feel unworthy of the greatness God has supplied.

By falsely believing yourself separate from and less than God you identified yourself as your personality and your EGO took over. But let me tell you - you have misinterpreted your own identity. You have misdiagnosed your situation. You are not your personality, you are God in human form expressing Himself through you with all the power to create and Love that he Has. You are a spiritual being having a physical experience experience.

To help you find your way back to the truth of your identity God gave you the EGO to use as a tool. The EGO is actually God's way of helping you identify what is God or Love and what is not. God/LOVE expresses itself as peace, kindness, patience, tolerance, compassion and beauty. The EGO expresses itself as greed, selfishness, violence, pride, guilt, vengefulness, spite, hate, jealousy and war.

The EGO is a gift given to us to help guide us to God

or Love. We know if we are going towards the EGO... we are going the wrong way. It's that simple!

What a miracle to have this built in compass! This roadmap. Did you think that God left you here on this spinning planet empty handed? Once again you underestimate God's Love for you or His commitment to you and your soul's sole purpose... TO FIND GOD, TO EXPERIENCE LOVE, AND SHARE GOD'S LOVE WITH OTHERS.

Your soul's sole purpose is to experience a heart, soul and life full of joy, creative expression, peace, love, happiness, contentment, health, wholeness and vitality. Given the importance of these goals, did you think that God wasn't going to help you? He is committed to this and will always be committed to this. Don't fight the direction that he is trying to lead you in. He's trying to lead you where you know ultimately in your heart and soul is where you need and want to go: home to Him.

You have been beating yourself up whenever you have been in EGO. Put down the bat and stop beating yourself with it. You have been "shoulding all over yourself." I should have done that, I shouldn't have done that. Stop. Just recognize that when you are acting from EGO you are not acting from God/LOVE. Remember this analogy

E.G.O. stands for Edging God Out.

Why does this happen to us? Why do we forget who we are? Why do we lose touch with our source and have to struggle to reclaim it the rest of our lives? I don't know. It is one of life's great mysteries. It's like asking "why does the body heal itself when it is cut?" It just does. I do know that God has planned it that way and as we follow God's map for our lives sometimes we just don't get all the answers. Sometimes we have to go on trust and faith whether we understand it or not.But remember, nothing happens in God's universe by accident.

PART ONE

MY DIALOGUE WITH God

Contrary Action

Chapter 10
-    Keeping The Focus On God

"EGO would quinymo ago meus vita tanquam illic est a Deus quod intereo ut expiscor illic isn't, quam ago meus vita tanquam illic isn't quod intereo ut expiscor illic est." "

I would rather live my life as if there is a God and die to find out there isn't, than live my life as if there isn't and die to find out there is."

Albert Camus

How hard is it to keep the focus on God? It is probably the hardest thing you will ever have to do. In this world we have so much distracting us from God: quick fixes and immediate "feel good" remedies for what ails us are everywhere we look. Fast foods, amusement parks, television, movies, sporting events, sex, etc.

Consider the time you have spent doing these daily activities and compare that with the time you have spent with God, focusing on God. You wonder why you don't have the real peace, happiness, comfort and joy you truly desire.

Before I stared writing this book, I don't think the hours I've spent communing with God would even add up to more than a day or two. I don't mean going to church or reading religious or spiritual books. I mean putting all things aside, sitting quietly by myself, going within and being silent with God. That is where you find God...in the silence within.

How much time in your life has been spent in silent communion with God? If it doesn't even add up to a day you've got some serious work to start doing. I know I did and still do. The communion with God never ends. So much of my life I wondered why I couldn't fully believe in myself. Why I wasn't truly happy? Why I wasn't being all that I knew I could be? In fact, I made so many of the same mistakes over and over and I seemed to be stuck in a place of disappointment in myself, knowing full well I wasn't being the person I was capable of being.

It's very hard to build a relationship with God when you have your focus on other people. Many times we are so caught up in our emotional "situations" with other people we aren't spending time with God. We have our attention on what other people are doing, what their behavior is and how it is affecting us and how they are disappointing us. We seek quick fixes to alleviate the pain we feel within. Instead we should turn to God, commune with God to heal our pain, and let our relationship with God turn our lives into experiences of joy, peace and serenity.

I can tell you personally that I have deviated my attention away from God so many times only to find myself confused, embittered and without faith. I have let so many things distract me from my goals, my ideas and what I think God wants from me. I have let other people's situations and needs become the primary focus of my attention, and when I have done this I have never been happier for it. I have always found myself saying, "I can't believe I just spent the last 4 years of my life on ...." When I was working on this book, recording God's communications with me, I got caught up in one relationship after another. Each of them different and demanding and I was more that willing to put my attention on these men to fix their situations, fogetting once again, my own purpose. I realized how hard it is for me to stay on track with my goals and ideas and how easy it is for me to be distracted.

To avoid this, you must put all of your effort and attention on God, while caring and giving to others. Whenever you find yourself out of this balance, you must quickly return yourself to God and to your own purpose.

Try this, put a note on your bathroom mirrior that says "God please help me be who you would have me be today." Then read it every day out loud while looking at yourself in the mirror.

PART ONE

MY DIALOGUE WITH God

Contrary Action

Chapter 11
- Trusting God

"Unus quod Deus planto a major domus."

"One and God make a majority."

Frederick Douglass

How difficult it is do to God's work, especially when it conflicts with what we want for Ourselves? We want this, we want that, but God wants this for us. How can I possibly give up what I want, to do something for some God's Will that I have never seen nor met?

You have seen God, have felt God and you have met God. You have seen God in every face you have ever come across. You have seen God in every glorious sunset you have witnessed. You have felt God everytime You have taken a breath, for it is the life of God that breathes through your body. You have met God each time a stranger has done something for you for no apparent reason.

Why do we stay in unhealthy relationships? Giving up a person or a path when it is not God's Will for us. You may feel painful because of the immediate loss, the sudden aloneness. Yet we are not really alone and God knows why he wants You and this person to be apart. Perhaps the person is going to do You damage down the road, damage that You can not foresee.

Perhaps the person is stifling your growth, holding You back in ways You can not identify. Perhaps there is more to learn from another person. Do you really think God created the entire universe but he can not direct You away from unhealthy people or situations towards more positive and healthy experiences?

Why do we continue to underestimate the wisdom of God? The power of God? How with all God's glory can we possibly put such limitations on His capabilities? Are we not floating around the universe on a globe, breathing, multiplying and experiencing life? God with His infinite wisdom and with His exceptional ability to create surely has the power to determine something as simple as what may harm You or help You.

We must trust God. We must be willing to let go of our will for ourselves and embrace God's Will for us. God holds the map of our lives in it's entirety. We may hold a piece occasionally, but when given a piece of the puzzle, the first thing we should do rather than try and interpret it with our limited abilities, is to ask God what it means and what God would like us to do with it.

Why don't we take direction? If our children came to us with a problem and asked us for a solution wouldn't their life be so much easier if they just took the solution and acted on it?

Instead they fight it, they think they know better (not seeing the whole picture), and they do their will no matter what. (Unless you have been fortunate enough to have children who simply behave, respect your guidance, and follow directions no questions asked. I doubt it!) This disobedience is exactly what we do with God. I don't mean disobedience as in Biblical terms. I don't mean disobey and be punished in hell. I mean listening to your higher intuitive voice. That's how God talks to you.

God steers us in directions and we fight them and go in other directions. He says go west and we immediately turn around and go east. We think we know best and then when we get into pain we wonder why? And worse yet, then we then blame God for it. We say how could God do this to me? Even worse, we say if there was a God, how could He let this happen to us? Yet weren't we the ones who didn't listen?

We also turn to Him and ask Him to help us out of jams and He lovingly does, guiding us in the correct way until His Will contradicts ours once again and the rebellion continues.

Surrender. Surrender, that is the word I say. Yes it may feel painful at first to do God's Will because we have to let go of what we want. What we think will be the answer to our problems. But when we surrender, we will get through that pain and into the promise of God's plan for us. This action MUST be taken on faith. Faith that God knows best. Faith that we are following Him into the Kingdom of Heaven, for that is where He truly wants to lead us.

We have a loving God, we must remember that. We have a God who loves us very much and wants us to experience a heart and a lifetime of Joy, Peace, Love and Abundance. Clearly, it is not His intention to lead us in to pain and despair, yet many of us must believe we have this kind of God. Maybe we have had parents like this and therefore we see God this way as well. Why do we put human qualities on God and try to measure His greatness by our own failed experiences?

God is Supernatural, more than our intellect can understand. We must trust that God has our ultimate best interests at heart and that we are merely His children and need to learn to listen and follow His guidance. He will steer us correctly if we allow Him to do so. Once in the land of God's Love, any pain we have been experiencing by trying to follow our own will, will no longer be present. It has been said over and over again in every spiritual teaching and religious writing: God's Will, not ours be done.

Lack, disappointment, confusion, sadness, emptiness, anger, and resentment are the conditions we experience when we turn from God's Will, from our highest version of ourselves. These conditions are killers and need to be avoided at all costs. Killers, literally, because they can cause disease in the body like cancer, heart disease, strokes, etc., and could end up destroying us. We destroy ourselves when we turn away from God and try to live a life without His help, guidance and divine direction.

Why choose these negative experiences when God offers us experiences of Love, peace, joy, harmony, health, abundance and happiness? Let God lead you. Surrender to him as a baby surrenders to it's Mother's breast. God will feed you with life sustaining and life giving sustenance, if you let Him.

PART ONE

MY DIALOGUE WITH God

Contrary Action

Chapter 12
-    Developing My Relationship with God

"You've got ut puto ut Deus est in imperium of vestri vita."

"You've got to believe that God is in control of your life."

Joel Osteen

Human beings are creative beings. We have the ability to create something new from nothing, to imagine something in our minds that has never existed and make it a reality. Whether it is flying an airplane, going to the moon, or building Las Vegas in the middle of a desert. Quite often it is simply influencing the daily events in our lives, an ability to create works hand in hand with God. We are co-creators together with Him. We intend something and the universe works together to manifest it for us.

We ask God a question and he manipulates the universe to provide us with the answer. I've touch upon this subject several times in this book. It fascinates me how God manipulates the universe to guide us and direct us. God is constantly providing us with information and signs. An unexpected run-in with someone who gives us the exact information we need. A phone call from a friend we were just thinking about. A TV show discussing a topic we were just contemplating. Do we pay attention to these signals from God or do we call them coincidences? People often say God doesn't answer their prayer. Doesn't he? Maybe we just don't have our eyes and ears open.

Are these "signals" chance occurrences or does God and the universe steer us and guide us as we go along through this "seemingly uncontrolled experience"called life? Funny, though, how everything has order and control i.e., gravity, the sun rising and setting, your heartbeat. Who is controlling all of that if not God? A car can be invented but to drive it someone must be controlling it. When something is moving, something else must be creating the force behind it. What could possibly be creating the force behind our movements? Behind our existence?

It is not us. Our brains are working. Our hearts are beating. Our food is digesting, yet we have nothing to do with it. Something else is controlling all of that. The brain?. Who is controlling the brain? How did the brain get created? So complex yet so precise. Is it one more event in a chain of accidental events?

When You create something as simple as a meal it's not created by a chain of accidental events. You have an idea, you go to the store, buy the ingredients, and prepare them. It takes work: planning, action and effort to create something. Imagine what kind of planning, action and effort must have gone into creating something so complicated, so precise and magnificent as a human being.

How do we underestimate our creator? How incredibly complicated the entire universe is and all it's workings, seen and unseen. Yet all working in perfect order masterminded by something. Random order would be one thing, perfect order is quite another.

To further illustrate, is there anything in your house or your life that You Yourself have not had a hand in creating? Your furniture did not get there by itself. Your clothes did not put themselves in the closet. Your children have not appeared by magic. You have a hand in all you create and God has a hand in all He creates. You did not create Yourself, therefore you must have been created. You know that obvious fact, but You can't physically identify your creator so You doubt His existence, therby undermining the greatness of God.

Someone else has created us and I call that someone God. God has created us with specific intention, purpose and direction. God had a specific outcome in mind when he created us, and You need to ask God to find out what His purpose for you is. God will tell you whatever you want to know. You must ask the inventor of something if you want to know the purpose of the invention.

I have learned that our purpose consists of things global and individual. However, don't think individual means not being connected to the whole. All things are connected to eachother and therefore affect the whole of everything around us: One another, other life on this planet, the entire universe.

Your actions, although they may seem to You disconnected and unimportant, greatly affect and influence the whole. There is no separation. It is, then your responsibility to put Yourself in right order with God and the universe. You must give up any isolated, in-grown, individualistic thinking and think for the good of the whole. You will be affected positively or negatively by someone else's choice regarding this as well. You will feel the brunt of each person's choice in your dealings with them. If they operate from self-centeredness, You will experience the pain of it and so too will they, if You are also operating from self-centeredness.

Choose to operate for the good of the whole universe in all matters: Politically, spiritually and environmentally. Your choice is extremely important and has profound effect on everything around You. Remember: everything is connnected. Do not underestimate yourself! God has created you. He has created great power in You and You are a remarkable force in this universe. You are very important to God!

It seems a human tradition to call out for God and all his glory when we are in trouble, yet many of us we doubt and underestimate him the other moments of our lives.

Our underestimation of God and of ourselves is the source of much pain. Our acceptance of His glory and greatness within us and around us is our freedom. That is our true road to happiness, joy and peace.

We are created in God's image and therefore also have the power to create and manipulate the material world. We can do this is two way: Our intentions can manifest results, and the words we speak about ourselves and life do become our reality.

My intentions, my oneness and understanding of my connection to the universe, has always been very strong. As far back as I can remember I've always had the ability to create the things I'm thinking about. I can make circumstances happen in my life by thinking about them. Many times in my life I have thought about things in specific detail and shortly after that they manifested. This always happens.

In fact, Oprah Winfrey invited me on her show on June 27, 2008 to talk with Louise Hays, Martha Beck and Cheryl Richardson about the Power of Attraction. I told Oprah my ability to manifest what I want has happened all of my life, longbefore I knew what to call it and sometimes is so strong that I have felt like a magician. Oprah said that happens to her as well. Cheryl Richardson called it "living in the core of peace."

Let me give you some examples of how I manifest. I had a friend named Sebastian that I had been very close to when we both lived in Los Angeles. He moved to Palm Springs and I hadn't seen him in years. Since his move we had talked only once and then I lost his number. Then I moved and my phone number changed. I called directory assistance in Palm Springs many times but his number was not listed. (This was before facebook) I had lost touch with a person who was very important to me.

One weekend some year later, I was going to Palm Springs and thought it would be great if I could somehow find Sebastian when I was there. I said to myself, deeply and clearly, if only I could run into him and get his phone number. Later that day after I had checked into my Palm Springs hotel, I took a walk and almost got run over by a jeep pulling out of a bank parking lot. I looked up and who do you think was in that jeep? Sebastian! Of all the streets in Palm Springs, he pulls out of a parking lot and almost runs me over. Unbelievable! How did that happen? The Power of Intention perhaps? Needless to say I got his number.

I'll tell you another story equally as interesting. When I was growing up in Connecticut, I was one of two bi-racial girls in town. There other bi-raical girl was Linda and she and I didn't really get on very well. Therefore, I was rarely involved with her, although we were about the same age, attended all the same schools and had many classes together. After I graduated from high school I never thought of Linda.

One morning I was in Los Angeles talking with a mixed girl who worked in a trendy clothing store. She asked me what it was like growing up mixed in the 60's and wanted to know about some of the difficulties of that. It turns out she and I had similar experiences and we were comparing "war" stories. For the very 1st time in over 25 years I thought about Linda. I wondered why I had never made a real effort to get to know her, understand her, or become friends with her.At that moment it seemed like a shame that I didn't and I could have. A mixed friend would have been good for me, and maybe both of us back then.

While I was driving home I wondered if I could get in touch with Linda. Maybe I could track her down through the internet. The next day after work I arrived home and listened to my answering machine. My Dad had called leaving a message. Now this was extremely unusual be-cause my Dad rarely calls me he as is always writing. The fact that he rarely calls me has been a major, I mean major, area of contention in my relationship with him. So needless to say, just the fact that there was a message from him was enough to knock me off my chair. But the second and most incredulous thing about that message was it's content. It said:

"Wendy, my girlfriend Reggie ran into Linda from your High School at her gym. She wanted you to have her phone number and asked that you give her a call. Her number is..." and my Dad proceeded to give me her contact information. Wow..

I believe God works with our intentions. Human beings have the ability to create and manifest that which we desire just like God does, because God is inside us and there is a part of us that is powerfully creative like him. These types of experiences have happened to me all of my life.

That's just a couple example of how powerful our intentions are and how responsive the Universe, or God is. Aligning your own intention- with God's intentions for you - is without a dobut the most powerful use of your intention. Then what you create is on the level of miracles. (Perhaps this explains Moses and the parting of the Red Sea.) I know how powerful God is and so I pray everyday for God to direct my life.

This is not how I have always lived. Often God was an after-thought. It was more like, oh yeah God, I forgot to include Him. Ooops.

I'll give you another example of how God uses the Universe to respond to Intentions. One time I wanted a job right down the street from my apartment. I absolutely did not want to drive in the crazy Los Angeles traffic anymore. I had been driving 20 miles to my job for the past year at Fox Television, but in L.A. 20 miles takes at least an hour, bumper to bumper. I wanted it to be on Ventura Boulevard within a few blocks from my house. I wanted it to be a Talent Agency and lastly I wanted the company to have only women. It was after Michel, so I was in my "I don't want to be around any men" phase. You can see I was very specific about what I wanted to manifest.

So where do you think my next job was? Right on Ventura Blvd where I had asked. The company was a powerful Talent Agency which coincidentally, only had women employeed there at the time. And to top if off, the universe gave me a boss that was exactly like my mother when I was a child. And not the good parts of my mother either, but the parts that hurt me and that I resented. So as a bonus, I got to do real work on some childhood issues I had with my mother by working with this woman. I would never in a million years have asked for that. But I was able to heal some of my relationship with my mother through working for this woman. See God's plan is immaculate. He not only works with you to create what you desire, but He goes further and thinks of things to add in that you would never think of. God is deep. The universe was working in conjunction with my creative thinking and it was perfect!

Many times people find themselves in situations that are difficult and don't realize they are in perfect situations to heal or learn exactly what they need. Many times God is working in our lives and we don't even recognize it. Remember this: There are no mistakes in God's Universe. You are exactly where you are supposed to be.

Now even though God had presented Himself to me in this way many times in my life, I still had not surrendered to Him and let Him guide me in all my ways. I was still fighting for control of my life NOT letting God run the show. But after many years of prayer and meditation, I strengthened my spiritual muscles and developed a relationship with God where I have learned to Rely on Him for everything. What I mean by that is, I think of Him like an electrical socket. I plug into Him and His energy carries me through the day. Going from Self-will to God's Will takes getting on my knees every morning and saying "Good morning God. Wendy reporting for duty. Tell me what you'd have me do today and where you want me. I am here to do it. Your Way be done not mine. I have no plans. Whatever you want God." And I still work on that surrender.

There are times I want to take my will back and act from Ego, or be selfish, and I do. But that lasts for such a short period of time now, because I get uncomfortable quickly when I am not in alignment with God, or what I know my highest self would do. If I find myself acting from my lower self, I quickly correct my actions.

So how do we get from having a belief in a God to relying completely on God? How do we get from lost faith or the understanding of God we had as children to a new understanding of God as adults? It's journey we are all here to take.

First we have to come to believe there is a God. And I don't mean a religious figure. I mean powerful energy, underlying all things that governs the universe. I'll tell you how I came to believe that. As I told you already I believed in a God, but I was in no way letting Him run my life. By running my life it doesn't mean I have no say in what I do. It simply means that when I say "okay God your Will be done, not mine" all of a sudden I start to have thoughts and feelings from a higher level. I start to think of the things

Love would do in a given situation. If I don't make that prayer, I am usually thinking less loving thoughts.

I used to think "letting God run my life" meant giving up my control, but that's not what happens. What happens is when you say "Your will be done not mine," God shows you a higher path you didn't see and you get to chose which path you want to take. You never lose control over yourself. You just have more choices. I have learned from taking the high road many times (when I really wanted to slap someone) that the high road is always better. God's loving direction always works out better for everyone.

IS THERE OR ISN'T THERE A GOD?

It all starts with making a decision about whether or not you really believe in God. You can't turn your will over until you make this decision, obviously. Here is how I did it. I read a book which said that "either God is or he isn't." It can't be both. You only have two choices. You have to make a decision one way or the other." Well that made sense to me. Obviously He either is or He isn't.

I thought about it long and hard and came to the conclusion that how the heck could I, a little person in this vast universe, declare there was no God. How arrogant would I be to think I knew that. I am one minute spec of being in an endless universe and I can't to speak for all and declare there is no God. So, since I had to choose either He is or He isn't - God won by default. My decision resolved that issue permanently for me. His existence was no longer a question. From now on I was going to live like there was a God.

Now coming to that conclusion didn't all of a sudden create a relationship with God that deemed me his servant. It simply got me started on the journey of building a relationship with God. At that point, I believed that God did in fact, exist. That is the first step to turning your life around and making a conscious choice to become closer to God, closer to who you really are and the God within you.

This decision is the first step towards realizing your true self and finding the peace in your life that you long for. So I say to you now: Make a decision. Decide one way or the other. "Either God is or He isn't." It can't be both. You only have two choices. Something cannot Exist and Not Exist at the same time. Decide for yourself what it is going to be once and for all. I did and it changed my life and put me on the path to God. Now it's your turn to decide.

If you decided there is a God, now you are ready to move on and develop your relationship with God. The second thing I did was I started praying to God right away, whether I could fully understand him or not. I forced myself to take A Contrary Action and I started praying to him everyday for His will to be done in my life, not mine. I started seeing results and soon realized Prayer really works. I pray, ask questions, He answers. I pray for Him to remove characteristics in me that are not loving and all of sudden I start seeing unloving behaviors and actions of mine I had never seen before so together He and I can get rid of them. He opened my eyes.

Part of the success I have in building my relationship with God is that I go to God directly and don't have to accept anybody else's interpretation of God. I don't have to believe in anybody else's ideas of God or any specific religious experiences of God, or rituals, or my childhood God or my parent's God. I have my own personal relationship with God. This is what Jesus himself did. When he came out of the desert after meditating, he went into the town and started telling people he had developed a personal one-on-one relationship with God and that everyone else could do the same thing that he had done.

Now that you are ready to pray to God, be ready to start getting some answers. It is your job to listen. God talks to me but not in a loud booming voice from above but in a feeling, or knowing, or thought that comes over me that wasn't there before. And usually I have not even come close to the kinds of solutions to problems or ideas of how to handle things that God comes up with. Every day start your day by praying to God and he will reveal himself to you and prove his existence in your life.

In the beginning, I forced myself to roll out of bed onto my knees and pray every morning, whether I wanted to or not. My prayer started simple and I repeated the same prayer every day, whether I believed it or not and things started to change. I'll tell you my prayer, or you can use your own.

My Daily Prayer

"God I offer myself to thee to build with as thou will. Release me of the bondage of self that I may better do thy will. Your will be Done God, Not Mine."

I also wrote down a few things I really didn't like about myself and started to ask God to remove them from me, because I didn't want to be that person anymore. I can't explain how it happened but those things I prayed to God to remove from me were removed. I said to God "I am selfish and self-centered and I don't want to be that way anymore. Please remove those defects of character from me. Thy will be done, not mine." As I prayed this prayer every day I started becoming less and less self-centered.

When we pray are we really having a spiritual experience with God? According to an article from Newsweek May 7, 2001, "Scientists have proven there are different brain circuits active, for example when Tibetan Buddhists meditate and Franciscan nuns pray. The question is what happens in our brains when we have encountered a reality different from, or higher than, the reality of everyday experience? The fact is our brain waves change when we meditate and pray. SPECT (single photon emission computed tomography) machines track blood flow in the brain.

The SPECT images are as close as scientists have come to snapping a photo of a transcendent experience. In their research Dr. Baime and Dr. Andrew Newberg at Penn State University discovered, as expected, the prefrontal cortex, set of attention lit up. The superior parietal lobe toward the top and back of the brain had gone dark. With no information from the senses arriving, the left orientation area cannot find any boundary between the self and the world. As a result the brain seems to have no choice but to perceive the self as endless and intimately woven with everyone and everything. "The right orientation area, equally bereft of sensory data, defaults to a feeling of infinite space."

Sister Celeste, a Franciscan nun, under went the SPECT scanner during a 45 minute prayer. During her most intensely religious moments, she felt a palpable sense of God's presence and an absorption of her self into His being. Her brain displayed changes like those in the Tibetan Buddhist Meditators, her orientation area went dark.

The fact that spiritual contemplation affects brain activity gives spiritual experience a reality that psychologists and neuroscientists have long denied. And explains why people experience ineffable, transcendent events as equally real as seeing a wonderous sunset or stubbing their toes.

The fact that a religious experience is reflected in brain activity is not too surprising, actually. Everything we experience, from the sound of thunder to the sight of a poodle, from the feeling of fear to the thought of a polka-dot castle, every experience leaves a trace on the brain. Dr. Andrew Newberg states, "the bottom line is there is no way to determine whether neurological changes associated with spiritual experience mean that the brain is causing those experiences ...or is instead, perceiving a spiritual reality."

I found this article to be very interesting and the research highly thought provoking.

Contrary Actions:

1) Either God is or he isn't. Make a decision one way or the other.

2) Even if you are not sure if there is a God, pray like there is and He will reveal Himself to you.

3) Pray everyday for God's Will to be done in your life, not yours. Watch the miracles start to happen.

4) Read "How God Changes Your Brain" neurosciene- tist Andrew Newberg's fourth book on "neurotheol- ogy" the study of the relationship bewteen faith and the brain. (Ballantine Books, 2009)

PART ONE

MY DIALOGUE WITH God

Contrary Action

Chapter 13
-    There is everything BUT happiness
     in this house!

"EGO don't teneo quis vestri fatum ero , tamen unus res EGO operor teneo : solus ones inter vos quisnam ero vere gauisus es qui have sought quod instituo quam ministro."

"I don't know what your destiny will be, but one thing I do know: the only ones among you who will be really happy are those who have sought and found how to serve."

Albert Schweitzer

What do you do when your house is filled with stuff, but not filled with happiness? Yes, you have a car, a nice house, trinkets, electronics and toys in every room. Your kids have their own TV's, cell phones, and video games. You have closets full of clothes, some you have never even worn. There are at least 2 cars in the driveway and if you live in America you really are spoiled rotten. We have every convenience afforded to us by the 21st century, yet something is missing. We feel empty.

No matter how much outside "stuff" we accumulate, we can never bring that stuff inside. It will always remain outside of us. No amount of "stuff" will ever make us feel fulfilled.

The saying "it's an inside job" really means that; you have to go within to feel your joy. That's where joy springs from. The heart is the well spring of love and joy. The heart is most alive when it is loving which means giving to others.

Of course, no one is saying it isn't wonderful to have nice stuff. I know I personally love nice things. I love Eqyptian Towels, 400 thread count sheets, a Mercedes, staying in nice hotels, having a beautiful house in the hills but remember the highest suicide rate in the United States is in Beverly Hills, California.

What does that tell you? Maybe it's depressing to learn once you have everything that money can buy that you still are unhappy. People probably feel hopeless at that point thinking there is never going to be a solution to that ache, loneliness and the hole inside that we all feel.

There is one thing I know: Happiness is something we feel inside and our deepest source of happiness stems from our connection with our highest self and our relationship with God. The degree to which we surrender and align our will with the will of a higher purpose, will determine the level of happiness we experience.

I think the late Pope John Paul II was a terrific example of how powerful and fulfilling a life could be when it is aligned with a higher purpose than the self and was in alignment with the will of God and based on service of the people on this planet.

I know how revered Pope John Paul II was and how many lives he touched. The turn out at his funeral was unprecedented. Even non-catholics were brought to their knees in humble gratitude for his presence on earth and the gift he gave all of us by sharing with us his devotion to humanity and to God.

A person like that moves people, inspires people and helps people see the goodness inside themselves and each other. Pope John Paul II was beloved by the world and the choices in his life demonstrated how powerful a person can be when their personal will is in alignment with being of service to God and following a plan greater than one's own petty and selfish needs.

Our purpose on this planet is to discover what is special about us and use it to serve others and contribute it to the world. When we do these selfless, or esteemable things, we feel good about ourselves. We feel self esteem from the knowledge that we are living right lives. That self-esteem creates happiness within, knowing we are serving God and our fellow human beings.

It is our own selfishness that creates the loneliness and hole within us and external possessions and belonging can never fill it.

Each of us must strive to bring our will into alignment with God's Will for our lives. In order to discover what that will of God is, we must pray for God to direct our thinking and give us knowledge of His Will for us and the power to carry that out.

The universe will begin to lead us in the direction we are meant to go. Coincidences, fortuitous occurences, and opportunities will arise to guide you. Take chances, try something new and walk in a direction that you know is serving other people. Whenever you have a chance to choose between selfishness and Godliness, choose Godliness. That choice will always create happiness and serenity within you.

Contrary Actions:

1) Try getting on your knees every morning and saying to God: "God I pray that you remove from within me every single defect of my personality that stands in the way of my usefulness to you and to my fellows. Give me strength as I leave from here to follow your Will. This is a prayer I say every day and it makes me far more conscious of others, and in deeper service to others. Also as I pray this prayer I renew my commitment to be of service to God and to my fellows, and I put my thoughts in the right mind set.

   It is a wonderful way to start the day, and after awhile of doing it you will see certain selfish elements of your personality start to fade away. God will do wonders with you if you ask him to! Remember though God is polite; He is a Gentleman. He won't kick the door in. He will wait patiently until you ask Him in!

PART ONE

MY DIALOGUE WITH God

Contrary Action

Chapter 14
- My Father

"Really valde populus planto vos sentio ut vos , quoque can fio great"

"Really great people make you feel that you, too, can become great."

Mark Twain

One day I had a profound awareness about my relationship with my father. God had placed me with my father to give me an opportunity to learn somethings my soul greatly needed to learn. He gave me a father who was a Master Teacher for me, but I didn't understand what I would eventually learn from my father, so I misinterpreted my father's purpose in my life completely. For years, I had a lot of resentment for him instead of Gratitude.

Recently I thought about one of my biggest flaws that had hindered me and held me back over the years: my inability to focus and exercise self discipline. Everyone knows in order to achieve something great, one must truly focus on something, putting all your energy into it disciplining yourself until it is done.

Before I surrendered to God, I was always scattered, starting things and not finishing them, jumping from one thing to another. Like many of us I was getting things accomplished just as long as I was believing in myself. As soon as I doubted myself, I almost always procrastinated, and made up reasons why I couldn't do something and, or would just give up on it.

I didn't have focus or self-discipline so here is how God works. As I have said previously, my father is a writer and as I was growing up he was completely obsessed with his work. His focus was so extreme, it was often at the exclusion of all others around him. He was self disciplined beyond comprehension. These attributes were grossly missing from my personality and truly I needed those qualities.

After I surrendered to God, I realized that I had been ungrateful throughout the years focusing on what I did not get, instead of all that I did get. I realized that my Dad had always been loving me every moment we were together. He was kind at all times. He listened to me so deeply when I talked and always offered me support and help if I needed it. My Dad was always reachable, he always came home, he paid all the bills and fed me, clothed me, and never laid a hand on me in anger.

He went beyond his perental requirements and bought a car for me when I was 19 and another one when I was 25. As a struggling artist, he sent me money to help pay my rent some years and even took me back in twice to let me get on my feet and go back to college. Every time I saw my Dad we laughed, held hands and he hugged me. My Dad told me he Loved me every time we talked. Others can not say all of this about their father.

When we did talk about his lack of involvement with me, I told him I felt neglected by his work. He apologized and said I was important to him, that I always have been, and that he Loved me. He said the thing he is most gratfeful for in life is that he didn't lose me or my brother to his writing and that we still loved him.

Yes, I had a lot to be thankful for and one thing is certain, I was Loved enough. But I couldn't see that for many years. I only focused on the times I didn't have his time, attention or interest, and because there was too much of that, so I worked it into a deep resentment.

This is an exampple of how people are complicated. I took his neglect of me personally. I deemed myself unworthy of love and attention, and felt unimportant and ignored as a child. I held a terrible amount of resentment towards my father and I had a negative opinion of my own worth .

One morning I said, "God I wish I could do what my Dad does. I wish I had all that concentration and that ability to push everyone and everything else aside and fully concentrate so I could accomplish my goals."

Then I had an A-HA moment! I realized that I had underestimated God, again. I realized that my Dad was a Master Teacher for me, who was there to give me what I needed more than anything. He was an example who had been placed in my life to help me learn and master the ability to focus and exercise self discipline. My Dad was showing me how to do it all along. He was meant to teach my soul the character traits it was desperately lacking and needed. Unbeknownst to him, he was exemplifying what I needed to develop in order to express my talents to their greatest potential. My father was serving God. Amazing. Everything happens for a reason and there are no mistakes in God's Universe. We can learn from everything.

I also learned people don't always Love us the way we think they should, but it doesn't mean that they don't Love us to the best of their ability. My father showed his Love in all the ways he knew how, and on top of that he was giving me what I needed most only I didn't know it. I learned so much from this relationship with my father and have since told him how grateful I am for all that he has taught me and for all the wonderful things he has been in my life. My Dad and I have always been able to talk about anything and everything. We alwys come to the conclusion that no matter what happens in life, no matter the mistakes either of us have ever made, or will ever make, we have loved eachother unconditionally and we always will.

God works in amazing and mysterious ways. We often have no idea how he is working and we forget to trust Him. When we underestimate or misjudge what God has created, or is providing for us, we get into trouble. Cannot

God determine what is best for us? Why do we keep trying to second guess God? When we don't accept things as they are and trust that God Loves us and knows what He is doing in our lives, we get into trouble.

We get into trouble when we are trying to hold on to things because we are familiar with them even when they are not good for us. We get into trouble when we continue to be angry at people for things they do when we don't understand what lessons they may be teaching us.

We cannot know what God has intended for us. We cannot know what the highest outcome is. But be assured God only has the highest outcome intended for us. The pain may confuse you, but sometimes pain is only there to get your attention. Therefore, always trust in God. Accept that things in your life have, and are, happening for a reason that God has intended and when you don't understand what God is doing Ask HIM and ye shall receive.

The answer: He is not here to let us down. He exists to celebrate and exhault us and we are here to celebrate and exhault Him and all of life. His workings unfold in the most complicated and yet the most simple ways. His works are magical. He is a Genius, an Artist, a Master Creator.

My father shared his heart, his dreams, and his passions with me everytime we talked, when we listened to music together or when he told me he loved me. My father makes me proud of all he has accomplished and the strong loving man he has always been. He has been my best friend in my darkest days, a voice of reason in confusing times, a place of stability and security that I could alwys count on.

I have been loved by my father, and for that, I will always be grateful.

But don't get me wrong, I do wish he would close his books and come out to California for a visit!

PART ONE

MY DIALOGUE WITH God

Contrary Action

Chapter 15
-    Who Are We?

"Quis nos es est God's donum nobis. Quis nos fio est nostrum donum ut Deus."

"What we are is God's gift to us. What we become is our gift to God.

Eleanor Powell

God is expressing himself as us and through us. God has already expressed Himself as every flower, sunset, animal, plant, star and creature in the universe. Within each of us is the heart of God waiting to express itself, just as in each rose seed is the rose waiting to express itself. We are creative beings, as He is, with all the power He has. We have the ability to manifest that which we desire from thought into the material world. The Universe is designed to help us accomplish that.

God has a plan for us that like the rose; He wants us to express the highest nature of ourselves. His tool: the Universe, gives us situations, opportunities, and people which lead, guide or help us express our highest self. We can hear this message repeatedly down through the ages and across religious lines. His purpose for us is clear – we are beings made of God here to Love like God.

God is a creative, intelligent energy, we can also call Him LOVE. The purpose of our lives is to express God's perfect Love for ourselves, others and God. All that is, is God. There is nothing else. All that is, is One.

When we are born we forget that we are in fact God. We believe that because we have individual bodies we are separate from God. We also falsely believe that because other people have individual bodies that they are separate from God, as well.

However, if we look at a brick up close under a microscope we will see individual cells. If we pull back we can see the brick is attached to other bricks and in fact part of a building or a lerger whole. The brick doesn't know this

People are all part of the same house of God and often don't realize this. No brick or person more important than the other. The difference between bricks and people is the bricks coexist peacefully, and people compare themselves to other people, try to tear others down, wanting to be the only one left standing and sometimes they destroy the house in the process.

A simple but useful analogy, Human beings are separate cells that together make up energy, a part of God. God can see the united energy of humanity. It is we who can not see this, except for the few enlightened Souls who know the truth of our oneness. They have told us this time and time again in various religions from around the world.

We are all God, created to express divine and perfect Love.

PART ONE

MY DIALOGUE WITH God

Contrary Action

Chapter 16
- God's Purpose For Our Lives

"Si nos did res nos es idoneus of , nos would stupendum ourselves."

"If we did the things we are capable of, we would astound ourselves.

Thomas Alva Edison

W hat does God want from us? There are those among us who attempt to teach us what they "think" God's Will is. They do so with a certain amount of wisdom until they get off course trying to impart ideas to you of specific things that upset God, and demand you believe or behave in a certain way to receive or experience the Kingdom of Heaven.

No human can tell you what God's Will for you is. They can give you suggestions, but it is only your direct conversation with God and asking His plan for you that will provide you with the answers.

Books can be written, ideas can be shared, churches can be built, ministers ordained and sermons can be laid out, but only you have the power to say to God: What is your plan for me? You then must listen to hear His answer. Look for signs all around you that express His answers for you.

No one else on this planet has His answer for you. Therefore, their ideas, religious customs, suggestions about what they "think" God wants you to do is speculation and often to be taken with a grain of salt. Of course if you Pray for God's Will for you and then begin to her the same answers all around you from different sources you may want to really pay attention to that. The Universe is probably telling you something.

It is up to you to turn to Him and ask Him what you are to do. You can read the Koran, the Bible, but you will not find your direct answers for you from God in these scriptures. You may hear other's testimonials of their experiences, Do not rely on the experience of other's to shape your relationship with God.

It is my opinion that any book you read that suggests you get silent, go within and meditate and asks you to go directly to God and give yourself to Him, following His Will for you is the correct way to find God. When one group or religion says their way or custom is the only way and denounces the ways of millions, that to me is not the Will of God. In the Bible it says, "Ask and Ye shall receive." I believe that.

I have read many books that tried to sway me in specific ways to believe this or believe that. And do you think each of these books has taken into consideration who you were and what unique gifts and talents you had to offer? Do these books know what God has intended for you?

Specifically, how can one sweeping generalization apply to the entire world when there are such diverse personalities and talents among people? Look around, it's obvious God is a firm believer in diversity, variety and color.

He is an artist in the truest sense of the world. His planet is filled with many different colors, species, and many paths all leading in one direction-to Him.

Turn to Him directly and receive His purpose for you. Your path may differ greatly from your neighbor but the goal and purpose is the same.. to elevate yourself and God to the highest level. To glorify His name and experience Him in You and You in Him. You and He are one and the same because He is all that there is.

God's purpose for us is often things we would never even think of. You may think you in a situation to learn one thing, and then afterwards find out it was to learn something completely different.

When we are dissapointed in people sometimes that is how we learn that it is only God we can count on and turn to for support. We can learn that God is all that matters and people can not and should not be counted on to provided for us what we need. People are temporary, God is Eternal.

We must take care of ourselves and rely on God, creating the life around us that God wants for us. That way when people disappoint us, as they often do, our emotional state is not thrown completely out of balance. This is important to realize.

We don't know what God's plan is for us during the experience, but we must trust Him and remember that He has our best interests at heart. Try to bless every situation as an opportunity to learn a lesson then let go without resentment and with gratitude for all that is learned.

PART ONE

MY DIALOGUE WITH God

Contrary Action

Chapter 17
- A Parable: The Three Trees

"Nemo alius in terra mos umquam polleo ludo persona Deus intentio vobis. Si vos don't planto vestri unique affero ut orbis terrarum, is won't fio."

"No one else on earth will ever be able to play the role God planned for you. If you don't make your unique contribution to the world, it won't be made."

Rick Warren

Once there were three trees on a hill in the woods. They were discussing their hopes and dreams when the first tree said, "Someday I hope to be a treasure chest. I would be filled with gold, silver and precious gems. I could be decorated with intricate carvings and everyone would see the beauty."

Then the second tree said, "Someday I will be a mighty ship. I will take kings and queens across the waters and sail to the corners of the world. Everyone will feel safe in me because of the strength of my hull."

Finally the third tree said, "I want to grow to be the tallest and straightest tree in the forest. People will see me on top of the hill and look up to my branches, and think of the heavens and God and how close to them I am reaching. I will be the greatest tree of all time and people will always remember me..."

After a few years of praying that their dreams would come true, a group of woodsmen came upon the trees.

When one came to the first tree he said, "This looks like a strong tree. I think I should be able to sell the wood to a carpenter," and he began cutting it down. The tree was happy, because he knew that the carpenter would make him into a treasure chest. At the second tree a woodsman said, "This looks like a strong tree. Should be able to sell it to a ship yard." The second tree was happy because he knew he was on his way to becoming a mighty ship.

When the woodsmen came upon the third tree, the tree was frightened because he knew that if they cut him down his dreams would not come true. One of the woodsmen said, "I don't need anything special from this tree so I'll take this one" and cut it down.

When the first tree arrived at the carpenters, he was made into a feed box for animals. He was then placed in a barn and filled with hay. This was not at all what he had prayed for.

The second tree was cut and made into a small fishing boat. His dreams of being a mighty ship and carrying kings had come to an end.

The third tree was cut into large pieces and left in the dark. Years went by, and the trees forgot about their dreams.

Then one day, a man and woman came into the barn. She gave birth and they placed the baby in the hay in the feed box that was made from the first tree. The man wished he could have made a crib for the baby, but this manger would have to do. The tree could feel the importance of this event and knew that it had held the greatest treasure of all time.

Years later, a group of men got in a fishing boat made from the second tree. One of them was tired and went to sleep. While they were out on the water, a great storm arose and the tree didn't think it was strong enough to keep the men safe. The men woke the sleeping man, and he stood and said "peace" and the storm stopped. And suddenly, the second tree knew he was carrying the king of heaven and earth.

Finally, someone came and got the third tree. It was carried through the streets as people mocked the man who was carrying it. When he came to a stop, the man was nailed to the tree and raised in the air to die at the top of the hill. When Sunday came, the tree came to realize that it was strong enough to stand at the top of the hill and be as close to God as was possible, because Jesus had been crucified on it.

The moral of this story is that even when things don't seem to be going your way, always know that God has a plan for you. If you place your trust in Him, he will give you great gifts. Each of the trees got what they wanted, just not the way they had imagined. We don't always know what God's plans are for us. We just know that His ways are not our ways. But his ways are always best.

- A traditional folktale, author unknown.

PART ONE

MY DIALOGUE WITH God
CONTRARY ACTION

Chapter 18
- How Do You Know
When It Is God's Will?

"Never locus a period qua DEUS has locus a to order "

"Never place a period where God has placed a comma.

Gracie Allen

What is GodS Will? It usually is the path you don't want to travel. It usually is the harder thing to do. It usually requires self-sacrifice and placing others before you. It usually feels like the thing that will not instantly gratify you.

Hearing God's Will can come through prayer, meditation, thoughts, imagination, synchronicity (the universe giving you clues) including writing such as this. But it is always a feeling, and inner knowinsg. It is the highest part of you communicating with the lower part of you suggesting one path over another. Your lower self responds to immediate gratification, material or physical pleasures. Your higher self or God self requires self sacrifice and non immediate gratification. Becoming aware of the difference between them brings you closer to identifying God's Will.

Some spiritual leaders believe you may be struggling with some of the same issues lifetime after lifetime. Whether you believe in life after death or not makes no difference. You will struggle with the same issues in "this lifetime" until you surrender to the will of God or your highest GOOD and highest purpose.

It matters not what your religious beliefs are or your specific affiliations. It matters not if you are Catholic, Christian, Buddhist or Muslim. The spiritual principles will continue to work no matter how you identify yourself. The world works the same for all people on it. Gravity does not apply to only a few. Repeat lessons don't happen only to a few and God doesn't speak to only a few.

      No human being can tell you what God's Will is for you. No religious leader, no group or deity. When you seek God you humble yourself before him, going down on your knees and praying to him asking for his will for you. Asking for HIM to guide you in all that you say and all that you do. Go to God first in all things. When you pray and meditate consistently the "universe," the mouthpiece for God, will give you signs pointing you in the right direction.

      Remember God's Will for you may not be God's will for someone else. We are not clones. Don't give people advice. We each have different roads to travel. You do not know God's will for anyone else. Stop telling other people what to do and get on your knees and ask what God wants you to do.

Contrary Actions:

1)   When faced with any choice or decision you need
to make, before you do anything else, get on your
knees and ask what would God have you do? Simply Pray for knowledge of God's Will for you and
the power to carry that out. Humble yourself before
God and sincerely desire an answer. Then get up
and go about your business. You have just placed
yourself in right relationship to God and the Universe. Now watch and listen carefully in the course
of the next moments, hours, days, weeks or months.
The magic will happen. You will begin to notice information is coming to you from the universe in the
form of books you happen to "stumble across", a TV
show that addresses a pertinent topic, people you
accidentally run into who happen to have exactly
the same experience you just prayed to God for
guidance about. God speaks through other people.

2.   Live as if only you and God exist. If it were only

you and God on this planet, who would you be? How would you be acting? How would you feel and think about yourself. Be that person!

PART ONE

MY DIALOGUE WITH GOD

Contrary Action

Chapter 19
- Christ

"Vos dico vestri a Sarcalogos?
Tunc satus acting amo Sarcalogos."

"You call yourself a Christian?
Then start acting like Christ."

Wendy Alane Wright

People have asked me to write about Christ. So I will spend a few moments in reflection about him. There have been many teachers on our planet, teaching us how to Love. Perhaps the most powerful teacher of all time was Jesus the Christ. I don't believe any other human being has ever reached the ability to Love that Jesus did. I'm inclined to believe that he was in fact supernatural. How else can we explain the level of selflessness he reached? Only God is that selfless, powerful and forgiving. However we define him: Human, Son of God, God himself - we don't need a final, complete and proven explanation in order to practice what Christ taught. Practicing what he taught I believe takes priority over arguing about who he was.

I have always known in the depths of my heart that we are here to love like Christ did. Christ came to teach us by being the perfect example of Love. He said if we love God the way He did, followed God's direction for our lives they way He did, and loved others the way He did, then we would enter the Kingdom of Heaven. The Bible says the Kingdom of Heaven is within. "Jesus saith unto him, I am the way, the truth, and the life. No man cometh unto the father, but by me."

Perhaps, this simply means we must learn to act,

think and love GOD like Christ did in order to find GOD and the "Kingdom of Heaven within." Jesus also said: "I am the light of the world. He that followeth me shall not walk in darkness, but shall have the light of life." Jesus came to earth to teach us all how to live a life that honors God. how to walk in the light. He taught us all how to sacrifice ourselves for the good of all. His example has left such an impact on the world that He is the most written about figure in history.

Unfortunately, people have forever twisted the message of Christ for their own personal gain. People have used Christ as a way to try to control and manipulate people. If you don't take Christ as your personal savior you will go to Hell for eternity. What a way to use fear to try and get people to do what you want them to do. I am leary of anything that uses fear rather than Love to reach me.

I think what moves people most about Christ, and certainly me, was his ability to love so deeply and unconditionally. Whenever people think about Christ himself, not the religion, we are humbled, awed and inspired. It's important not to get caught up in an argument about whether he was the Son of God or not, although I believe He was. It is more important to master his teachings and apply them to your life. It is time to stop the religious warfare and exemplify all that Christ stood for.

Christ led a humble, simple life and encouraged us to do the same. He spoke about compassion, unconditional love, tolerance and forgiveness. He fed the hungry, clothed the needy and healed the sick. Christ was not for religion or religious causes. He was against them. He believed` you can have a one on one relationship with God, forget the priests, and the trappings and go directly to God. He introduced this teaching as an alternative to the established religions of the time. This was unheard of and threatened the power structure of Judaism. He was killed because of his resistance to the religious establishment.

Forget the politics surrounding Jesus' death though. Forget the controversy regarding his identity. Rather focus solely on his Message and Teachings. Study what he said, How he lived his life. What he instructed us all to do. In Matthew 5:43-48, Luke 6:27-28 Christ said Love your enemies, do good to those who hate you, bless those who curse yiou, pray for those who misetreat you."

Don't get caught up in religiosity. It is always flawed due to the weaknesses of humanity. There is so much discourse in interpretations of the Bible and it's meanings throughtout the world and over the centuries that I feel more comfortable studying only what Christ said and did, goimg directly to God and leaving it at that.

Embodying the Characteristics of Christ will lead us all to peace within ourselves and a relationship with God that can only be known through Love. Jesus came to teach us how to stop being selfish and instead, called upon us to sacrifice ourselves for others. It was the main theme of his message: Get rid of our self-will and take the higher path of selflessness and sacrifice. Christ said: "Beloved, let us Love one another. For Love is of God; and every one that Loveth is born of God, and knoweth God. 1 John 4:7)

That is much different than what the Christian religions often try to tell us when they say only people have have accepted Chirst as their Lord and Savior can know God. Christianity, the religion, doesn't always reflect what Christ the man said.

I believe Christ was a pacifist. After the Roman Emperor Constantine converted to Christianity in A.D. 312 and began to conquer "in Christ's name" Christianity became entangled with the state, and warfare and violence were increasingly justified by influential Christians. I think human beings always twist the messages of Christ for whatever advantages they feel they can get at the time.

I believe that we are all here to evolve into a being that behave and acted with love and compassion like Jesus did. I believe he is our best example of what we, as human beings, can be. That is if everything they say about Him is correct. I usually struggle with information in the Bible because so much time has elapsed since it was written and so many people translated and interpreted it. Did you ever play the game telephone? It is a simple children's game. Ten people or so sit in a circle. One person says a sentence into the ear of another, then that person turns and says it to the next person sitting next to him, who in turn says it to the next person sitting next to them until they have gone all the way around the circle. The funny things is that by the time you get back to the beginning of the circle, the sentence is nothing like the one that was orginally spoken.

I fear that has happened with religions, with Christ, with the Bible, etc., and so I do not count on any human writings as the final authority. I have questions and doubts about different things, but I am not waiting for complete understanding to happen before I begin to try to emulate Christ. I am spending my life right now trying to be more loving, compassionate and forgiving like Him every day and in every situation I experience. In all situations, I ask God for guidance and ask "What would LOVE do?" I know one thing, the seed of God is planted inside each and every one of us. If we ask God for answers they will come.

Contrary Actions:

1)   Get on your knees every morning and say "God I want to be more like Christ. I am selfish and self-centered please remove these qualities from me, I don't want to be that way anymore." I have done this consistently for many years and I have become less and less selfish and self centered.

2)   Stop arguing about Christ and start being like Him.

3)   Don't think less of yourself, just think of yourself less often. Go feed the hungry, volunteer your time at shelters, be a big brother or sister, adopt a child.

4)   Christ forgave his crucifiers. Forgive someone you never thought you would forgive.

5)   Study Christ. Read about Him. Ask God to help you know Him better.

CONTRARY ACTION - PART TWO

2 II

OUR RELATIONSHIP WITH OURSELVES

"Laboro vestri own salus. Operor non pendeo in alius."

"Work out your own salvation. Do not depend on others."

**Gautama Siddhartha
(Buddha)**

PART TWO

MY DIALOGUE WITH God

Contrary Action

Chapter 20
- What is Wrong With Us?

"Lacuna motivation doesn't opus. Is mos plumbum ut a vita - porro negotium of tendo pango mihi. Perceptum ut appreciate quis vos have quod qua quod quisnam vos es."

"Deficiency motivation doesn't work. It will lead to a life-long pursuit of try to fix me. Learn to appreciate what you have and where and who you are."

Wayne Dyer

Ll my life I have tried to figure out what is wrong with me. I always thought there is more to me than this. I am supposed to be and do more.

I would read spiritual books and I would agree whole heartedly with the spiritual ideas presented there. I would feel spiritual, begin speaking spiritually but I never finished the books. I read them half way and was on to other things. I never stopped and did the work of applying the principles in my every day life and in every moment of my existence. However, a part of me deep inside wanted to experience the results of peace, tranquility and the oneness with God I knew the work would bring.

I wanted to know surrender and was angry that I didn't have that already. I mean why should we have to work at those things? Why aren't those just the gifts that God gives us? Why do they take work and sacrifice? I wanted to know how to become like the spritual people I admired. I wanted to become all these wonderful spiritual things and not have to work so hard t do so.

That was my dilemma. I felt in my soul that the purpose of life was to become these great things, but I was not willing to work too hard at them. I would mediate for 20 minutes and feel proud and spiritual. I would feel a connection to God, a oneness, but then it would be months, maybe years before I would meditate again.

I was a spiritual "wanna be", a spiritual misfit. Lost, looking to be found. I had great intentions and a clear understanding that God was Love and that our closeness to him was our purpose and the divine expression of him as me was my intention. However, I was not willing to work for any of that - until the recovery movement.

When I got to the recovery movement, I became willing. I was willing to work at applying those principals in all my affairs. I was willing to clean up my act. I started to listen and I developed a hunger for that. I no longer had to be the center of attention and have everyone listen to me. In fact I would rather they didn't, and I would rather listen to them.

At first there was still a desire to have people like me, but also I developed a deeper interest in who people are and what they are about. I became fascinated at watching how people treated each other. For the first time in my life I stopped being so concerned with me and started noticing how other people behaved. How they talked to each other, opened doors for each other, bent over to help some one pick something up that had been dropped. I noticed a whole world of kind acts, an infrastructure of people helping and caring for each other in ways I had never noticed before. It was amazing.

If the answer to God is to sit quietly, meditate and allow God to speak to us then all this running, hiding, seeking, speaking, thinking, moving and mental masturbation is just a waste of time.

Our continual search as human beings for more, more, more: more money, a bigger house, more power, more fame, more friends, more things, more luxuries, more toys more, more, more is just a waste of time.

Ask the very rich. They have a lot more than most people will ever have. Often celebrities say they know something is missing because they have everything worldly thing and yet still felt empty. Yet we spend so much time looking for the answers outside of ourselves? Society has conditioned us to think this is what we have to do. Marketing is directed to making you believe that you will finally be someone if you have this or that product. That their product will make you better, stronger, faster, more worthwhile.

Many of us are now slaves to the things we have sought to fulfill ourselves. We work around the clock in jobs we don't like to keep ourselves in the things that don't fill us, or lead us to God.

If you understand that God is in us and he is in

everyone and everything and that our purpose here is to know God completely, then we all need to go within, go to the silence. Sit still, stop seeking, stop moving, let go of that desperate pursuit of material things. As the Buddha said, "maybe you want for too much."

How can we overcome society's pull in the wrong direction? The commercials, the materialism, the capitalism the seemingly never-ending need for humans to be more, have more, travel faster, and farther. Those outside things will never get us closer to God, to peace, to Love. We already have everything we need, we already are God. All we need to do is to be still, to be quiet, to be one with God.

I don't have to work hard at this at all. Becoming more spiritual and a master of my relationship with God isn't as hard as I thought it would be. Maybe it is the easiest thing in the world. It requires me to pull up a pillow, sit down on the floor and sit still. Know nothing, do nothing, say nothing. It is the easiest job I will ever have to do. Of course, isn't that what the great masters have been saying all along? I got my wish. I get to be more like the people I admire and it's not that hard to do! Sit still and meditate. I can do that.

Moya K. Mason said in her article "Christianity: Its Sojourn in the Desert, The Lives of Our Desert Fathers

and Mothers, hundreds of years before Christians seques-
tered themselves in the Egyptian deserts, the young Buddha fled his family and kingdom to find peace in the forest.
He dismissed the inequities of the Indian caste system and
proposed a religion based on asceticism, poverty, and de-
mocracy. A life of simpler needs would help in the search
for oneself and peace. The Hindu Brahmins also lived in
the solitude of forests, existing on leaves and roots, in a
solitary quest for deliverance. The Old Testament tells the
story of Moses meeting God in the desert, and this gave
the desert a sacred quality for Christians ever after. Centuries later, St. John the Baptist became a hermit in the
wilderness around Jerusalem, as did Jesus, who went in
solitary prayer or took friends and disciples to find peace
and to pray to God. As Peter F. Anson writes in The Call of
the Desert, The solitary life led by John the Baptist in the
Desert of Judea [and Jesus' sojourns into the wilderness]
served as the inspiration for countless Christian hermits
in after ages. " It seems human beings have been searching
for an inner truth, for answers to their deepest questions
throughout the centuries. And yet the questions remain."

What's wrong with us is we spend far too much time
looking for our happiness, peace and answers on the outside. We need to look inside.

PART TWO

MY DIALOGUE WITH God

Contrary Action

Chapter 21
- ### Your Past Does Not Define You

"Perago sulum dies quod fio per is. Vos have perfectus quis vos could."

"Finish each day and be done with it. You have done what you could."

Ralph Waldo Emerson

Often people think because they haven't done something before that they never can. That is not true. The future is an open book with pages that have not been written yet. Your past does not define you. Each day is a new day. You have a clean slate and an opportunity to be whatever you create yourself to be. As a child you were excited about the next day. You never knew what tomorrow would bring. You didn't want to go to sleep at night and miss anything. When the next day came you were open to any possibility, acting spontaneously on opportunities that presented themselves to you. One of the kids in your neighborhood would say lets go play ball and you would say okay and run off with them, being fully present in the moment.

Now we are adults and we think and over think everything, too afraid to be bold and to take chances. We are no longer living a spontaneous life filled with joy, but a carefully thought out life lived in fear. Our attitudes have changed. We have become defeated from too many painful experiences, disappointments, unmet expectations and our own analysis of what we think about everything. These voices are so loud in our heads it makes it hard to live life freely. We live as if we already know the outcome to situations before we even enter into them.

But what do we really know? We know what hap-pened yesterday, but we have no idea what will happen later today or tomorrow. What we "think" we know is based on our perceptions that have been colored by our past ex-periences. Five people can have the same experience and have five different experiences of that experience. (The way we interpret what happens to us is as much a part of the experience we have had). I always say that each one of us wears a pair of colored glasses that we view ourselves and our lives through.

The color of our glasses is absolutely determined by the things that have happened to us and how we have in-terpreted those things and what we have made them mean in terms of ourselves, and the world. If we took those glass-es off we would see things very differently. If we put some-one else's glasses on we would see things very differently. We must always remember that we do wear glasses. That what we think about life is simply a judgment we make about it.

Remember this too, the way peple treat you has noth-ing to do with you. What they see through their glasses is runing their lives. It all about them, not you. What if we could take the glasses off and see everything anew? What if we could see life through the eyes of a child again? Before we made so many judgments and had so many opinions about what was happening to us? What if we took off these "all knowing glasses" and didn't know what was coming next or what everything means. You see that is reality for us. We really don't know what is coming next or what will happen or what everything means. We don't have all the answers, but we act as if we do.

The fact is you and I don't know how tomorrow will turn out. Tomorrow can be anything we want it to be. It hasn't happened yet, so we don't know. Anything else is a lie, a fantasy you have made up in your mind.

We are going to have to take off the glasses of your past experiences and all the meaning we have given to them and start looking at the world again like the wonderful, unwritten journey that it really is.

You may have failed yesterday, but that does not mean you will fail today or tomorrow. You may have been in relationships that haven't worked before, but that doesn't mean the one you are in now or your next one won't work. Life is what YOU make it. It really is. It takes courage to take off those glasses which seem so comfortable now and see life anew. When you do that, it's called a paradigm shift.

Here is a story about a Pardigm Shift

A man was on a crowded subway sitting looking out the window, while his three children were running all over the train. The children were out of control, making a lot of noise and bothering the other passengers. Yelling and screaming up and down the aisles, spilling people's drinks, ripping newspapers out of people's hands, hitting each other and being extremely obnoxious.. The father was just sitting there looking out the window. He wasn't disciplining his children. It was as if he didn't care. People were looking at the man, making faces at him, gesturing to him about the kids hoping he would do something to stop these kids from causing so much disruption. But the man just sat there as if he was oblivious and ignored all the people's comments.

Finally, a woman who couldn't take it any longer, went up to the man and said in a very irritated tone: "Sir, Your kids are running all over the train and disrupting everybody. Why are you just sitting there?

What the hell is wrong with you?"

He looked up at her slowly and said in a voice that was almost inaudible, "we just came from the hospital. My wife just died and I don't know what to do to help my kids right now."

The woman felt ashamed and took the man's hand. She was suddenly embarrassed, apologized and asked if there was anything she could do to help. She had shifted all at once from angry to compassionate. She had sympathy for the man and now it made sense why he was just sitting there.

This is called a paradigm shift. You had one too didn't you?

A Paradigm shift is when we get new information that shows us a situation is not what we thought it was. That is the truth most of the time. Most situations are not what we think they are because we never have all the information in any situation. We must always remember our judgements are based on incomplete information and realize we always have room to grow and to see things differently. We are not stuck with our old perceptions of things. We are not stuck in perceptions about who we are and what we are capable of

We couldn't possibly know what is coming today or tomorrow. So now that you remember you can't predict tomorrow based on what you thought about yesterday, you should also realize you can't predict whether you'll fail or succeed tomorrow.

What is stopping you from stepping out of the box, taking off your glasses of what you "think" you know about yourself and life and being open to seeing life as if everything is brand new and anything can happen? Even wonderful things!

If you have a goal, go for it! You can't predict in advance how it will turn out or whether you will succeed or fail. So many people stay stuck in the same old boring story day after day never changing what they do until they get in a rut aand depressed wondering what happened to their lives and dreams. I'll tell you what happened. They got complacent, they gave up, they believed they knew all the answers, and just stopped trying. They stopped seeing each day as a fresh new slate just waiting for them to create whatever they wanted to create.

Tomorrow can be anything you want it to be and

that's the truth. You are not defined by what you have done in the past or mistakes you have made before. You are new everyday, reborn. Don't let a misconceived definition of yourself linger into tomorrow. Whatever you were yesterday is gone. Today you are new and anything is possible.

Children when learning to walk don't say well, I couldn't walk yesterday so I probably can't walk tomorrow. I'm gonna fail, so I just won't try." Children don't say, "I have never ridden a bike so I probably can't and never will." An adult might not have owned a business yesterday but he or she might own one tomorrow. You may not have all the money you want in a bank account today, but you might have that amount in the future. Life is what YOU make of it. You have been given the power to create and manifest whatever you desire.

Is there something in your life that you always wanted to do? Have you talked yourself out of a dream that was very important to you? Do you dream of achieving a goal but just can't see yourself in that role? Have you been comparing yourself to others and measuring yourself against them? Stop doing all of these things and take off those colored glasses once and for all!

Contrary Actions:

1) Take a moment and write down 3 things you have always wanted to do. While making your list try to let go of any limitations or doubts that may try to creep into your mind. Write your first thoughts quickly.

 a) - _____

 b) - _____

 c) - _____

2) Now write down the reasons that have started to enter your mind about why you can't accomplish those 3 goals. No matter how silly they sound, write everyone of them down. List them quickly because they will come at you quickly. We are going to get them out of your head and onto paper so you can see exactly what thoughts are driving your life and keeping you stuck. This is part of becoming conscious in your life and doing this exercise and writing things down will help take the power out of the false statements in your head.

a) - _____

b) - _____

c) - _____

d) - _____

e) - _____

Need more room? Get a pice of paper and keep writing.

3)   Now look at your list. What are you telling yourself right now? If you are like everybody else that voice that sabotages you just threw several reasons at you for why you can't do it. This is how the human brain works. First, you will have a great idea and then the next thought will be why you can't accomplish it, i.e., not good enough, don't know how, never have before, aren't smart enough, haven't ever achieved anything that big before, and on and on. The difference is, I am going to help you get through that. The list above are the lies you are telling yourself. Tomorrow isn't here yet. These thoughts aren't true. These are limited thoughts generated by fear. Imagined fear of events that

haven't taken place. You couldn't possibly know what tomorrow will bring for you. The truth is you can do anything you want to do. You have to stop listening to those voices in your head that are not based on fact and are there only to keep you stuck.

Every human being has these voices, even the most successful people. It is just part of the human condition. What successful people realize is the voices and thoughts are not reality. They have learned to accept that they are there, just part of being human and they do what they dream of doing anyways.

Take off those glasses filled with the perceptions your mother had of you, that your father had of you, and any negative beliefs you have about yourself. Take those glasses off and see your life again through the eyes of the child within you. Your life is new and full of possibility and tomorrow you can create, be, and do, whatever you want. Get into the now. Stop living in yesterday. Today is a new day. Anything is possible. Tomorrow is your's for creating.

What you do today will lay the foundation for the life you want to live tomorrow. If you start today taking baby steps towards achieving one of your three goals, you will be one step closer to it tomorrow. As Wayne Dyer mentions in his fantastic book Wisdom of the Ages: "Just start, don't even think about finishing the project or how overwhelming the task may seem. Do nothing more than begin. Seize the minute.

Put the book down right now and seize the moment. Place a bookmark here, and when you have begun your project, return to your reading. What you will discover is Johann Wofgang von Goeth's meaning of 'Boldness has, power and magic in it."

Thomas Edison's famous remark "Genious is 1% inspiration and 99% perspiration. Seize the moment. That 1% is the recognization of your thoughts and feelings. To actualize the genious that you are, you must MOVE to begin the implementation of your inspiration."

Often what stops us is the fear we won't get it right, that we won't do it good enough, or that we won't do it perfectly. Guess what? You don't have to fear perfection because you will never reach it. None of us will. Perfection is reserved for God. Instead just do the best you can and when those three things on your list are done start a new list.

4)   Now, pick one thing off your list and start taking some action towards it.

PART TWO

MY DIALOGUE WITH God

Contrary Action

Chapter 22
-    **Making Conscious Choices**

"Aiunt ut vicis changes res , tamen vos vere have muto lemma vestri."

"They say that time changes things, but you actually have to change them yourself."

Andy Warhol

We have to choose and take responsibility for our choices and our actions. In order to be happy with other people we need to find happiness in ourselves first. If you feel a hole within you and you can't seem to fill it, that is because it is a God sized hole. Only God can fill it. Without God it is hard to find real contentment and to love yourself fully, or bring your best self to any relationship. That is why so many realtionships fall short or fail.

Relationships get all messed up by the baggage we bring from prior relationships with others. We dwell on who didn't give us what we needed and we feel sorry for ourselves. We must accept the fact that people can never give us eveything we need. They have never been able to. Only God can do that. We need to focus our energy and attention on connecting to God, loving ourselves, valuing who we are, valuing the good in us. We must choose to intentionally stop acting on the bad in us. Know that what you focus on you create.

If we focus our thoughts and energy on all we never had, all we didn't get we'll just get more of it. We'll also wallow in resentment towards others we will be victims in our own lives. However, if we focus our thoughts and energy on how amazing we are, how deserving we are, and treat ourselves with Love, respect, and care, we will create a much better life for ourselves. The saying "we are what we eat" is true and so is the saying "we are what we think." In order to have a loving relationship with ourselves we need to think highly of ourselves. We have to know who we really are, who God says we really are. If we knew how awesome we really are, who God created when he made us, there is no way we would say or do the things we do to hurt ourselves and others.

So the question is how do we change what we think about ourselves, our past and about others? The answer is we change our actions and that changes our thinking. We can not change our thinking without changing our actions first. It's like we have to start eating fruits and vegetables and drinking more water in order to start seeing healthy results in our body. It's the same with our actions in relationship to God, ourselves and other people.

If we consciously choose to take the action of talking to God, spending one-on-one time with God in prayer and Meditation, we will come to know God the magnificent creature God created us. If we consciously choose to start taking care of ourselves physically, we will start to think more highly of ourselves and feel more valuable. If we consciously choose to be more helpful to others, we will begin to feel more useful and have a higher regard for ourselves. When we develop a higher regard for ourselves, we will naturally make choices that are good for us. It all begins with our actions.

You can not think your way into feeling better about yourself, being closer to God and about being more useful on the planet. You must act your way into these changes. Life is all about Action. This book is about Action. You can not just read it, you will have to take some actions in order to change, to grow. When we start to feel deserving of good things, we can choose to stay away from things that are not good for us whether it is people, food, chemicals, conversations and experiences.

So how do we make this transition from where we are now to where we want to be? From who we are now to who we want to be? Who we really are? We have to learn For example when we are learing to ride a bike we have to learn balance. Balance is not something you can explain and then suddenly you understand and then suddenly have it. Balance is something you have to experience for yourself. There is no magical, no overnight solution. First you get on the bike and then you fall off. Then you get back on the bike and then you fall off, again and again, until eventually you learn how to balance yourself on the bike.

Then you learn to ride in a straight line, drive the bike up hill, down hill, jumps curbs and maybe even do wheelies if you are daring, and pretty soon you are one with that bike.

So it is with getting to know God and with loving ourselves. We have to take an action - a simple one such as waking up in the morning getting on our knees and praying to God. You have to consciously choose to do this every morning if you want to get closer to Him. You have to spend more time with Him.

You can wake up every morning, look in the mirror and say to yourself: "I Love you and today I will do what is best for you." And yes, you will make mistakes during the day. You will make a wrong choice or fall off the bike, but you will get back on and stand in front of the mirror the next day and say: "<u>I Love you. You are important to me and I value you. Today I will do what is best for you.</u>" Eventually, by consciously choosing to take this action everyday you will start to think more highly of yourself and feel more Love toward yourself.

Now this is a process of taking many new actions so it may feel weird at first. So what? Taking new actions takes some getting used to. They may be things you have never done, but to get something you have never had, you have to do something you have never done.

Holocaust survivor Viktor Frankl said, "we who lived in concentration camps can remember the men who walked through the huts comforting others, giving away their last piece of bread. They may have been few in number, but they offer sufficient proof that everything can be taken from a man but one thing: the last of the human freedoms -- to choose one's attitude in any given set of circumstances, to choose one's own way."

We have a choice each and every day as to who we are going to be, in all circumstances. One of the biggest choices for me is how I under eat or over eat. I starred intha ABC reality show Fat March in 2007. For 5 weeks I had to consciously alter my behavior, exercise regimine and diet. I walked from Boston to the New York State line, 205 miles! It was an amazing acomplishment. I was on the show for 5 weeks until I got a foot injury and was forced to go home.

Since returning home I have slowly become more-conscious of what I am eating and how much. I am also applying Contrary Actions to my eating habits.

I have to say I loved being on TV. It was fun to watch the show with my daughter and my husband when it aired! We shot much of the show in my home state of Connecticut and some right in the town where I grew up. I even got to see my father one day. Coincidence? I think not!

PART TWO

MY DIALOGUE WITH God

Contrary Action

Chapter 23
- Becoming More Than We Are

*"Adveho visio ut visio per vestri own limita-
tions, tunc reperio a via ut pulsus preteritus
lemma."*

*"Come face to face with your own limita-
tions, then find a way to push past them."*

Unknown

Do you have goals you want to accomplish but haven't as yet? Do you want better relationships, better health, more money, more friends, more happiness? Of course you do. We all do. So how do we get all that we really want out of life?

The answer is that we have to do different things than we do right now. We have to let go of old thoughts and take new actions that will restructure our lives. Our old ideas may have worked at some point in the past, but now they only keep us stuck.

We have to take new actions, ones we have never taken before. If you want what you've got, keep doing what you're doing. If you want something you've never had, you have to do something you have never done. What we do today will show in tomorrow's results. Today is a good day to start taking new actions. If we do nothing different now, then guess what? In six months when "later" shows up, nothing will be different. If we want to drive a Mercedes next year then we better do something different today so when next year shows up, so will the Mercedes.

People "say" they want to change but keep doing the same things they have always done. Then they wonder why things never change. People hold on to their old ideas for dear life, afraid to let go of what they know because they are afraid of the unknown. These fears plague people. The funny thing is though, if you try new ideas and they don't work you can always go back to your old way of doing things. Just pick up your old ideas they aren't going anywhere.

I've watched my second ex-husband struggling with an issue that has haunted him for years. Every time we talk about it he clings to his position, defends his beliefs, owns them with all his might and by doing that he owns his problem too. The fact is, from that stance, there can be no change because changing his position about it will require that he change his thoughts and ideas, and he is unwilling to do that. He is more committed to having the problem than having the solution.

Even though his thinking causes him pain, he is more familiar with the same old thinking than with new ideas, and people would rather be in "familiar discomfort" than in the unknown.

Why is it so frightening to change? What are we afraid is going to happen to us if we let go of our old thinking and ideas? Think back to when you were growing up. You have always tried new ideas throughout your life and it's turned out pretty good so far. Let me give you a few specific examples: Walking. That was a new concept to you at some point. Talking- that was new. What about riding a bike? Writing? Going to school? Driving a car? Moving out? Getting a new job? Having Sex? Weren't all these new actions at some point in your life?

The fact is we have constantly been changing and allowing new ideas to become a part of who we are. We naturally are familiar with change and very adaptable to it. We resist change as we grow older for fear of the unknown, yet all of these unknown examples have worked out fine. They were not familiar behaviors to us, but once we acted on them, we got used to them, and they eventually became automatic. With each new change we became more than we were previously. We risked making mistakes along the way and we didn't beat ourselves up over it. Now as adults, we beat ourselves up when we make mistakes, and we are afraid of being embarrassed and not looking good to other people. Why? Nothing has changed. The learning development process is still the same now as it was when you were a child. We learn through mistakes.

When you were learning to talk or walk you made some mistakes. Are you still beating yourself up over them? No, of course not. You don't even remember what they were. Mistakes are just part of the process of learning. They are not a value judgement of your worth.

Why when we aspire to be more than we are or to accomplish something we have always dreamed of, do we get stuck in fear and refuse to take new actions? Instead we sit around wishing we were something more. We spend years wasting our lives afraid of failing, afraid to change and afraid of making mistakes.

We have forgotten that mistakes are just part of the process. We can never learn something new without making along the way. To me making mistakes isn't scary, staying the same is scary. Change isn't painful, it's the resistance to change that is painful. Being haunted by disappointment in ourselves for not taking risks, for missing opportunities, that is scary. Not realizing our potential that is scary to me.

In the field of medicine, if a group of scientists are convinced that there is no cure for diabetes and then one day new research shows that several cases of diabetes have been cured, new tests would have to be conducted right? It would be a mistake for the scientists to stick to their old ideas, to defend them or be unwilling to change. It would be their job to determine the truth and investigate the evidence and accuracy of the new findings.

The fact is we are changing all the time. We are always learning new things and making them a part of our world. We have new technologies like Cellular Phones, Computers, Internet, DSL, Air Bags. New theories constantly replace old ones. Guess what; the world is round not flat! That took some convincing but now it's just a fact that everyone accepts.

We obviously have a lot of changing to do if we are not where we want to be in life. What we are doing right now is not working. Incorporating new thoughts, ideas and actions into our lives is necessary for us to evolve. We can't be afraid to change, to be wrong or to make mistakes when it comes to our own lives, goals and dreams. We can't be afraid to look honestly at ourselves and make some changes in who we are being. We must be open to new information about ourselves if we are going to grow.

Years ago I knew someone who had 19 failed relationships. I know because I was the 19th. He blamed the women for all the problems in his relationships. He didn't see that his own stubborness, insecurity and fear of intimacy chased them away. He believed his ideas were "right" and wouldn't listen to any alternative views. He was afraid of the truth, so sadly he stayed stuck in his own misery. Those 19 women have gone on with their lives, and he probably is still a victim of his own stagnant thinking. Although I hope not. Being "right" doesn't always mean you win.

I embrace the truth as an opportunity to grow and become more than I already am. I pray everyday for the willingness to be open about myself, the courage to change and to take new Contrary Actions. Fear has very little place in my life. The truth sets me free and that suits me just fine.

I agree with american billionaire Richard M. Devos when he said, "the only thing that stands between a man and what he wants from life, is often merely the will to try it and the faith to believe it is possible."

Contrary Actions:

1)   Look in the mirror each morning for 7 days and
        say to yourself " I am honest, open and willing to
        change."

2)   Write down 3 things in your life that you "desper-
        ately" want to change about yourself or a circum-
        stance in your life.

A.

B.

C.

3)   Then write down 4 steps you can take for each one
        that will help you change yourself or that situation.

4)   Take those steps.

5)   Be Gentle with yourself. Remember, it takes a little
        change at a time, one day at a time, to end up with
        an extraordinary life that you are proud of.

PART TWO

MY DIALOGUE WITH God

Contrary Action

Chapter 24
- What is Working and Not Working in Your Life

"Maximus res est is : Potum procul ullus moment facio quis nos es pro quis nos could fio."

"The important thing is this: To be able at any moment to sacrifice what we are for what we could become."

Charles Dubois

Everybody has areas in their lives that are either working or not working. Even the most succesful among us. Life is not perfect. In order to create a life that has more of what you want in it and less of what you don't you must look honestly at your life and the areas that are not working and change them. You cannot fix a problem if you can't admit there is one. In order to call a plumber and fix a leaky pipe in your house, you must first admit there is a leaky pipe. If you don't admit the pipe is leaking you will be up to your ankles in water and the leak will cause damage which will get worse the longer you ignore the problem.

It is the same with each of our lives. There are areas that simply don't work. It may be in the area of our relationships, job, finances or our health. It's important to take an inventory of your life so you can see what needs to be changed. Don't beat yourself up over what is not working. None of us were born with a manual for life. We are improvising this thing all the way.

We are all growing, and as the French-Cuban author Anais Nin said, "we do not grow absolutely, chronologically. We grow sometimes in one dimension, and not in another; unevenly. We grow partially. We are relative. We are mature in one realm, childish in another. The past, present, and future mingle and pull us backward, forward, or fix us in the present. We are made up of layers, cells, constellations." That being the case, we need to take an inventory of our growth on a regular basis.

If your life was a business, let's say a grocery store, you would regularly take stock of what was fresh and not fresh on your shelves. You would honestly look at your merchandise and throw away any damaged or open containers, throw out rotten produce and replace the old items with fresh ones. You would not beat yourself up in this process. You would simply make the changes. It would do you no good to pretend the items on your shelf were fresh.

It is the same with your life. It does you no good to deny the truth to yourself. You have to look honestly at your life to see what is and isn't working, so you can throw out the bad situations, toxic relationships, spending that is irresponsible, a job you are unhappy with or bad eating habits that are causing you harm and replace them with fresh ideas. You don't need to beat yourself up over this. You simply need to love yourself and make different choices that work better for you.

Any company reviews it's employees, productivity, marketing strategies, income vs. spending, investments and makes changes wherever applicable to get better results. Why do we do less for our own lives?

You must take an Inventory of what is and what is not working in your life and make changes wherever they are needed. Your life is at stake. So let's get started!

Get a piece of paper and divide it into three columns:
1)   What is working.
2)   What is NOT working.
3)   Solutions, i.e. Contrary Actions.

For this exercise you will need to get conscious. Get honest with yourself. The goal is to start designing the life you really want. Until you admit there are problems with your current design, you will never replace the curtains or the carpet.

In column one write down all the things about your life that are working, big and small. The things that are making you happy. Then in column two, write down all the things you are frustrated with, people you are frustrated with, situations that you would like to change in your life. Be very honest. It's okay, this is just an exercise. Take all the time you need. Be easy on yourself. Everyone has things in their life that are not working including the most successful people in the world!

Now title the third column Solutions/Contrary Actions. Make a list of possible solutions to each item you listed in your 2nd column as not working. Try to think of things you have never done, things that may be scary to do, things that are down right unreasonable and seem almost impossible. Look where you can set some boundaries. Remember this is your life. You are responsible for creating the life you dream of and remember that what you are doing now is not cutting it. So think outside what is familiar to you. Stretch yourself.

Listen, doing Contrary Actions won't feel comfortable at first. In fact, they may feel down right uncomfortable. Changing your life is not about being comfortable. Making changes may be uncomfortable at first, but the end results will give you the quality of life and workability you are searching for. Your uncomfortable now, why not be uncomfortable doing a Contrary Action that is going to increase your level of happiness?

Contrary Actions get easier with time. In fact, they become new habits and a part of who you are. Soon you won't even realize you are taking Contrary Actions. With repetition they will become your normal way of acting.

Remember God made you a one-of-a-kind blessing,

never to be repeated, with tremendous power to chose and design the life you dream of. Make your plans, goals and strive to fulfill your dreams without fear, but do it with faith and trust in God. Embrace every amazing moment you've been given. Take your hits and get back up. If you lose a leg, learn to hop. If you lose a hand, learn to write with the other one. If you lose at Love, pick better next time and keep your heart open. We have to keep going in life. Don't make excuses for yourself or others.

Think big. Don't sell yourself short. If you can envision it you can do it. Believe in yourself. No one else will believe in you the way you can. Surround yourself with people who Love you. Make lots of friends. Love yourself. Love God and remember how deeply God Loves you. Give this life everything you've got!

Contrary Actions:

1)   Pick any one of the Contrary Action/ Solutions in your 3rd column and do it.

2)   Break your Contrary Action down to baby steps. Do small baby steps, not giant leaps. Baby steps get you where you need to be safely and consistently.

3)   If you start and then get off track, don't beat yourself up. Just continue on with your Contrary Action. When learning to walk you fell alot. At what age did you give up on learning to walk?

4)   Get up and do one of the solutions on your list right now! Make that phone call, look for a new job, apologize sincerely, forgive someone. Do what you need to do to improve the quality of your life.

PART TWO

MY DIALOGUE WITH God
Contrary Action

Chapter 25
-    Changing Your Life, Taking
     a Personal Inventory

"Lying ut ourselves est magis penetranter ingrained quam falsidicus ut alius."

""Lying to ourselves is more deeply ingrained than lying to others"

Fyodor Dostoyevsky

When the pain of your situation gets to be too great you'll be ready and willing to change YOUR behavior and choices that are causing your pain. That's right it's YOUR thinking, behavior and choices that are creating the life you have. No one else is responsible. If we are living a conscious life, than we have to accept the fact that we have freedom of choice to create our life as we want it to be. If we are in emotional pain then it is our own choices that are causing our lives to be painful.

I am not talking about circumstances out of our control, like earthquakes, tornadoes, freak accidents or unfortunate tragedies. I am talking about the circumstances in our lives that we have some control over such as choice of relationships, partners, jobs, our goals and dreams, and whether or not we do what ultimately makes us happy.

Often in my life I found myself in painful relationships and wasn't willing to look at what I was doing or choosing that was causing me pain. When the pain caused by my own choices became too great, I decided to live a conscious, responsible life and take back my power. I was no longer willing to live my life from situation to situation and wherever the wind blew. I began making specific conscious choices about what I wanted my life to be like. I decided

I wanted to be a kind, considerate and loving person no matter what people around me were saying or doing. I also decided I wanted a loving and healthy relationship with a man or no relationship at all.

No more of the dysfunctional painful relationships I had always "chosen." Although, if you had asked me a few years ago I wouldn't have seen how I was responsible for creating that dysfunction. I finally found a great tool for taking an honest look at my life and the choices I had made. After doing a particular exercise, I saw that I was the common denominator of all my relationships. I made a list of the four men I had relationships with in the past:

Rob   Francis   Michel   Jeoly

Under each of their names I wrote down everything they did to hurt me. Then I turned the page over and wrote their names down again and listed everything I did to hurt them. Looking at my list of my behaviors and reactions I suddenly realized two things:

1. My behaviors and reactions were the same in every relationship. They were five different men with completely different personalities and flaws, but I was the same in each relationship. For the first time in my life I was looking only at my behavior and how it was part of the problem.

2. Also, I realized that it was my reactions to the people and situations in my life that had caused me the most pain and problems in my life. My choices and reactions were making my life unmanageable.

I decided I wanted to change those behaviors on that list and NOT be that person anymore. I decided I wanted to be a even more kind and loving person no matter what other people did. It was a very conscious choice. I took many Contrary Actions to achieve it, in fact my choice to take many of the Contrary Actions in this book are responsible for the miraculous changes in me. I was willing to look at myself honestly and do the work it took to change myself. Now it's your turn to look at you.

Contrary Actions:

1) Grab a piece of paper and write the names of the people you have had important romantic relationships with. Stop reading and go get the paper and something to write with. Go in a room by yourself, close the door and take 10 minutes to do this. Now under each of their names, write down everything they did to hurt you. Don't worry if you get upset. Cry if you need to, but just keep going. Now turn the page over, write their names again and list everything YOU did to hurt them. This will take some real honesty here, so get honest. More honest than you have ever been.

Now you have some crappy things under what they did to you. There is no denying that. But for the next 10 minutes I want you to keep your focus on what you did to them. This is the thing most people never do. Look at your list. Is this who you want to be? Are there any behaviors on your list that you don't like? Good, you can stop them. From now on in your life keep the focus on you, your actions and your behaviors. Work on changing the things on your list. Forget for now about what they did. You can't change them. You can only change you. Changing YOU will bring YOU more peace, serenity and happiness. I want you to congratulate yourself for getting through this exercise. It is a tough one. Now you deserve to pamper yourself a bit. get up and give yourself a treat, a hot shower, a swim, chocolate and then continue reading.

2)   Get another piece of paper. Make 3 columns: (1) Situation Causing Me Pain, (2) What am I doing to cause this? (3) What Contray Action can I take - in Baby Steps? Now proceed to fill in column 1 by making a list of the areas in your life that aren't working or are causing you pain, i.e., not having enough friends, bad relationships, excess weight,

poor finances, stalled career, etc.

Here is an example:

Column (1) Getting A Degree

Column (2) Haven't gone back to school. Told myself I was too old. Made excuses.

Column (3) Choose a school. See an admission counselor. Register for classes. Attend classes and follow though to completion.

Looking at this list will not provide you with new information. But creating this list means you are addressing these areas of pain in your life and you can be proud of yourself for that. Many of the solutions you have thought about before, maybe even for years. NOT taking these actions has been YOUR part in causing the pain in your life. Your choices cause your pain.

Don't beat yourself up about this. You have done enough of that. Be gentle and loving with yourself. Life is about progress not perfection. You aren't going to get life "right." We will never be perfect and that's okay. Always remember you are human, making spiritual progress. Progress, not perfection is the goal. We will make good and bad choices, procrastinate, daydream, make excuses. So what? There is NOTHING wrong with you. You are whole and complete.

Today you can make a different choice and consciously choose to create a new reality for yourself. It's time to be satisfied. You are not too old, too fat, too tall, too smart, too stupid or too late! If you want to have something you have never had, you can have it by doing things you have never done. It's that simple.

Today, you can decide to take baby steps in the direction you really want your life to go in. Now that you have your list of Baby Steps, get moving and set some reasonable time limits. Be easy on yourself. You are not going to leap from where you are to where you want to be. You don't have to take giant steps, just baby steps. They will get you there too. You can take small, Contrary Actions, (baby steps in a new direction). You are on your way to living a conscious life. Pat yourself on the back. Not everybody gets this honest with themselves. You are very powerful.

PART TWO

MY DIALOGUE WITH God
Contrary Action

Chapter 26
- ## Love Yourself

"'When vos reperio pacis intus vestri , vos fio quidam quaedam quedam quidam alio quisnam can ago procul pacis per alius."

When you find peace within yourself, you become the kind of person who can live at peace with others."

Peace Pilgrim

Y ou have to love yourself before you can have true happiness inlife, before you can have a true union with someone else. You know the saying, "you have to love yourself before you can love someone else." Whey do people say that and what does that mean?

Well, first of all, when you really love yourself that means you respect your own needs and put your energy into things that result in your highest good. It means you know how to say "yes" to things that are good for you and "no" to things that could harm you.

Loving yourself means you know yourself. You know know what you want and what you don't want in your life and you honor that. You trust your instincts and listen to your own needs. You care about yourself.

Loving yourself also means making you important to you. People may come and go, and experiences will come and go, but you will be with you all of your life. You must practice loving yourself and become a master of it. Learning to love yourself is necessary before you can offer that kind of respect and love to others. If you have no idea how to love yourself, how are you going to love someone else? You cannot transmit something you haven't got. When you love yourself you will be capable of giving healthy love to other people.

How many relationships end in divorce? When we don't know what we are worth, or what we really want in a mate, we often settle, seeing people for who we hope they will be, rather than who they really are. Or we think they will change, or we can change them, and we end up in a relationships that don't work with people we don't really like. It is important to have romantic relationships but the most important relationsips are with God and yourself first. All other relationships must stems from that.

We have to choose to love ourselves. Many people came from homes where, for so many different reasons, we didn't get the love that was needed. We didn't learn how to love from our caretakers and we are left wounded, battered, and bruised and brokendown by childhood. But those early experiences do not determine our value, God does. Those experiences don't have to determine what tomorrow brings. Tomorrow isn't here yet, it is a blank canvass and we have yet to paint it. We are the artist and the skye's the limit! Don't ever let your past determine your future. That is like saying you ate Cheerios as a child so you have to eat Cheerios the rest of your life. Who says so? If you don't want to eat Cheerios anymore don't ever buy them again. When someone offers them to you say no. It is the same with anything.

A few years ago I decided I wanted to know peace. I wanted to be my best and live from love and from my highest self consistently. Since I'd never done that, I realized I would have to do things I had never done before in order to have something I've never had. I learned I had to let go of certain people who were toxic for me, who really didn't have my best interests at heart. And it was painful and sad but pain is sometimes the cornerstone for growth and pain happens in some transitions. Even transitions from pain to peace can be painful. You have to trust in your inner self, and if you are praying and following your instincts and walking through the doors that God opens, then you must have faith that if God brought you to it he will bring you through it. When you don't have faith, and fear has you paralyzed, start to pray every day for faith and God will help you develop it.

I always heard the saying: water seeks it's own level and wondered how that was true for me. I always attracted men that were afraid, and I mean afraid of everything in a big way. Afraid of people's opinions, afraid to let people see their body, afraid of abandonment, afraid of not being good enough. Paralyzed by fear they were. That was the common thread that ran between them. But I couldn't figure out how their fear was anywhere near my level of fear.

Granted, I had some fears, but I didn't have that many fears and certainly I wasn't paralyzed by fear.

Then one day I realized that I had focused all my life on fixing other people and that it was because I was too afraid to focus on myself. My huge fear that I had which made water seek its own level was not the same fears they had but the level of fear was the same. I was so paralyzed by fear of facing myself and making myself a priority in my own life that I would attract other fearful people. The fear in me was as strong as the fear in them but we didn't fear the same things. Strange how that answer just came when it did and not one second before I was ready to receive it.

So now that I know on a subconscious level I draw that to me which is at the same level. It makes sense to assume that I have to raise my water level if I want to attract higher levels of water or "higher quality people", people closer to the sunlight of the spirit, closer to the God within them and not people stuck in fear and EGO, which to me means Edging God Out.

I needed to raise my water lever and I began that by taking my attention off everyone else and focusing on me. In other words. I began to "mind my own business" and pay attention to my own prayers, mediations, needs, activities, what makes me happy, what creates peace for me, my friends, my body, my goals and my daily life. I minded my own business and got out of other people's business. I still did volunteer work and charity work but I worked hard to put my own spiritual house in order first, so I would be able to have healthy relationships with others.

Love yourself first so you can love another. "You cannot transmit something you haven't got." I love that saying. How can you give love if you haven't learned to love yourself? I used to hear that and that you can love others and not love yourself. But really, how good are you at loving if you haven't mastered it with yourself? How much do you actually know about what valuing someone means if you haven't experienced what if feels like to value yourself? If you have experienced personally what valuing yourself means then you will be able to value others. If you haven't personally experienced valuing yourself, then you are just guessing at what valuing someone else means. And I mean valuing someone in a healthy way, not a co-dependant way- loving someone in a respectful way with boundaries.

If you don't know what those things feel like first hand from experiencing them with yourself, how will you know how to transmit them to someone else? It is like teaching someone else how to make an omelette, yet you've never made one. You will be so much better at showing them if you have experienced it yourself and have perfected it to some degree. My point, love yourself first, get good at it and then you will be able to love others well too. As the Buddah said, "You yourself, as much as anybody in the entire universe, deserve your love and affection."

PART TWO

MY DIALOGUE WITH God
Contrary Action

Chapter 27
- Overcoming Fear

"Condita erroris est secui of dues unus pays parumper plenus vita."

"Making mistakes is part of the dues one pays for a full life."

Sophia Loren

"Virtus est non absentis of vereor, tamen dominatus of is."

"Courage is not the absence of fear, but the mastery of it."

Mark Twain

For most of us, our biggest problem in life is fear. Our own fears stop us everyday from becoming who we really want to be. There are two kinds of fear. One is an instinctual fear that stems from situations that are actually occurring to us in the moment. Physical, tangible events that are real threats, such as being mugged, being in a car accident, being in a building that catches on fire, in a hurricane, a tornado, etc. This fear is nature's way of keeping us on alert to harmful things, an instinct that protects us and instructs us to protect ourselves.

The second kind of fear is imagined. There is no imminent danger, you feel fear but it's all in your head. It sounds like this: What if? What if I get in a car accident? What if my plane crashes? What if I am to old to do it? What if they don't like me? What if I fail? What if I try and people laugh at me? What if I am not good enough? What if I am not worth it? What If...ad finitum. We have an on going dialogue of imagined fears in our heads constantly telling us we are not good enough or we are not going to make it. Therefore, one of our goals in life is to learn to tune these voices out and we can do this by taking "Contrary Actions" that prove these fears were never real.

You are very familiar with imagined fears. Scenarios running through your head that keep you from going out there and following your heart, dreams and ideas. We all suffer from Imagined fear. We worry about future events that haven't even taken place yet! These are obviously not primal fears geared toward protection, rather they are fears that are holding you back, keeping you from being who you really are. These kinds of fears you must work through if you are to be successful, if you are to be happy. Anyone can do it, but it must be a conscious choice that you make.

Here is a simple acronym:

F.E.A.R stands for =
Fantasy Expectations Appearing Real

An extremely handy tool to have is remembering to 'keep your head where your feet are." If you are driving in your car worrying about something two weeks from now that hasn't even happened yet, and you are feeling anxious about it, stop. Reel your head back in from fantasy land. You just went on vacation...from reality. Keep your head where your feet are. Look at your feet, see where you are. Talk to yourself, "I am in the car, I am driving down the street, there is a green house with blue shutters on my right. I am on the way to the grocery store. I see big white cloud. That lady has a pink shirt on. Get your mind on what is really happening. So much of our time we spend thinking about stuff that isn't even happening. We take little vacations into fantasy land and then get all upset up about our "little trips." We have got to learn to get into the moment.

Listen, whenever we try something new fear accompanies it. Remember learning to walk? Well probably not, but if you were too afraid to fall you would never have learned to walk. If you were in fear of tripping, running into things, or stumbling, you would have quit trying to learn. Our drive to walk is so powerful we don't even think about what could happen to us. We are so focused on our goal we don't notice the fear.

That is how we must deal with fear in other areas of our lives. We must stay so focused on the goal, take Actions, even when we don't want to, and don't quit until we have achieved our desired results. Imagine if someone said to you; " Okay, you've tried to learn to walk long enough, stop, no more falling and stumbling around." At what age do you give up trying to learn to walk? Never. You just do it until you can. So it goes with anything you want to achieve in life. Just do it until you can. Fear does not have to stop you. Fear is just part of our learning curve. <u>Failure is when you take your focus off the goal and put it on all of the reasons you fear you won't get there.</u>

We all have a hundred forms of imagined fears such as fear of failure, fear of success, fear of being judged, fear of rejection, fear of the unknown, fear of not being good enough, fear of making a mistake, fear of not looking good, and so many others. Our fears keep us stuck in the same patterns and behaviors year after year.

As William Shakespeare once said, "Of all base passions, fear is the most accursed." I honestly believe fear is the most debilitating of all emotions. You can never get over fear by trying to talk yourself out of it. The only way to get over fear is to walk through it, to do the things you are afraid of - take a Contrary Action. That's how to get the courage. I once read a great book called "Feel the Fear and Do It Anyways" by Dr. Susan Jeffries. I recommend it for anyone struggling with fear in their lives. Okay, that's most people so she should sell a heck of a lot of books!

Dr. Jeffries's book was one of the greatest books I have ever read because it is all about the concept of taking action even if we are fearful. Most every new experience we have in life is accompanied by some kind of fear. Many people let fear hold them back from what they really want to do in life. They let fear hold them back from saying things they really want to say or expressing themselves in some way or another. People can waste their entire lives waiting for fear to pass, or trying to find the right way to talk themselves out of feeling fear. You can't talk yourself out of feeling fear. You will always feel some fear, it's a part of being human. There is nothing wrong with you. it's your job to can feel the fear and take the action anyway. Eventually, the fear subsides after you take actions and soon you may experience no fear at all in that particular situation.

Of course when you try something new and unknown, you will feel fear again and repeat the process. You must practice walking through fear if you are to become all you can be and all you are meant to be. If you are determined to have excellent relationships, friendships and true vocational satisfaction you must train yourself to walk through fears. Success does not happen only to certain kinds of people. Being successful in life can happen to anyone. It can happen to YOU, if you choose it.

What you need to understand is that successful people feel fear too. Many people falsely believe that successful people are not afraid. This couldn't be further from the truth. The fact is they are often more afraid because the stakes are higher. They are playing a bigger game. The difference is they walk through the fear and they get to the other side.

I remember former Mayor Rudy Guliani of New York

City talking about fear one day. To paraphrase, he said he didn't experience fear when speaking in public anymore, but when he was asked to sing at an event, he was terrified. He was violently ill in the bathroom before he went on stage. Mayor Guliani was a public speaker for years. He was afraid? Sure. Anytime you try something new you will experience varying levels of fear. Fear is a perfectly normal and acceptable part of being human. It is common and normal and that will never change. What has to change is YOUR relationship to fear. You must accept that it will always be a part of your life and not let it stop you.

Success doesn't mean you have to measure yourself against any other standard of accomplishment made by others. Your success comes by overcoming your own barriers and fears and achieving more than you were capable of achieving the day before. You become a master of Contrary Action in your own life. Your greatness depends on how well you take Contrary Action and walk through your own personal fears. Whether it is in your relationships, with your children, family, career, hobbies, personal goals, dreams, finances, fitness or health, taking Contrary Action will take you as far as you want to go. There is no magic potion or secret knowledge for achieving success, anyone can do it, including you.

So to reiterate because it's that important- Successful people take courageous actions even though they experience fear. They do not let fear stop them, they just accept that it comes with the territory. When they have a goal they experience fear, but continue on in spite of the fear. In fact, they experience all the same fears of people who are not taking actions. They have fears of not succeeding, fear of being judged, fear of not being good enough, fear of making mistakes, fear of failure etc., but they don;t let those fears stop them. I hope I am driving this home loudly enough because if you get this one principal and apply it to your life, your life will change drastically.

We experience fear whenever we lose control of the outcome of something. I used to spend my entire life trying to control people, places, things and events because I didn't want to be hurt by them. I think most of us are just trying to avoid the experience of pain. However, to have a fullfilling, successful life, we must accept that pain is sometimes part of the process

I'll tell you a story I know about a butterfly.

A man found a cocoon of a butterfly. One day a small opening appeared. He sat and watched the butterfly for several hours as it struggled to force it's body through that little hole. Then it seemed to stop making any progress. It appeared as if it had gotten as far as it could, and it could go no further. So the man decided to help the butterfly. He took a pair of scissors and sniped off the remaining bit of the cocoon. The butterfly then emerged easily, but it had a swollen body and small shriveled wings. The man continued to watch the butterfly because he expected that, at any moment, the wings would enlarge and expand to be able to support the body, which would contract in time. Neither happened! In fact, the butterfly spent the rest of it's short life crawling around with a swollen body and shriveled wings. It was never able to fly. It needed the struggle of exiting the cocoon to give it the strength to survive and fly. Without the struggle the butterfly crawled off to die.

(author unknown)

What the man, in his kindness and haste did not understand, was that the restricting cocoon and the struggle required for the butterfly to get through the tiny opening were God's way of forcing fluid from the body of the butterfly into its wings so that it would be ready for flight, once it achieved its freedom from the cocoon.

Sometimes pain and struggle are exactly what we need in our lives to become strong enough to soar. The sooner we walk through fear and do that which we are afraid of, the stronger we will get, the less afraid we will become, and the better we get at overcoming our fears. You have things right now in your life that you really want but there is fear standing in your way of getting them. It's time to get past it.

Concept:

Successful people feel fear too. The difference between people who do, and people who just think about doing is people who are doers feel the fear and do things anyways." They take Contrary Actions. That is how people achieve greatness. You must practice feeling your fears and taking actions anyway. Wayne Dyer said, "there is no scarcity of opportunity to make a living at what you love; there's only scarcity of resolve to make it happen." I want to help you make it happen so here is a brief exercise developed by Molly Gordon, author of the book "Getting Free From Fear" that I want you to do.

"Make a list of all of your fears, writing as fast as you can to block the internal censor. Include EVERY fear, however small or irrational. Then read them aloud, suspending judgement. Notice that being afraid does not have to mean losing ground. If it feels comfortable, share your list with a friend. Before sharing your list, explain that you simply want a witness, that you are playing with how it is to acknowledge your fears without being pulled off center by them. Be clear that you are not asking for help and that you do not need advice. You do not need to be fixed. Ask your friend to simply listen, and to acknowledge you for being conscious of your fears."

First of all, I want to acknowledge you for doing that exericse. It takes a strong, courageous person to look at their fears and be willing to work toward walking through them. I am very proud of you. Now let's move on to the next Contrary Action to help you get past a few of the more specific fears you have that may be blocking some of your goals.

Contrary Actions:

1). Make a list of five things you really want to do but are afraid of i.e. sky diving, having a new relationship, leaving a current relationship, going back to college, starting a business, making new friends, running for office, whatever is weighing heavy on your heart.

2) Write the fears you have that are blocking your goals or limiting your relationships, accomplishments or any other area of your life. If you are going to get past them, you first need to know what they are. So take 10 minutes and figure a few of them out. Are there a few big ones that spring immediately to mind?

a) - _____

b) - _____

c) - _____

d) - _____

e) - _____

Knowing the human mind, you probably have a lot more than 5 excuses or reasons floating around your head telling you why you can't do them. Write as many of these thoughts down as you can think of. Get them all out and onto a piece of paper. You can take some of the power out of them if you can see them.

Whenever I have problems in my life and feel overwhelmed, I write them all down. Once they are on paper almost by magic they start disappearing. I look at the list a week or two later and all of the issues I had been upset about have been handled.

3)   Pick one of your goals and start on it today.

4)   Read "Feel the fear and do it anyways." Then feel the fear and do it anyways ...no matter what.

5)   Share your fear with others. It often dissolves once it is not a secret.

PART TWO

MY DIALOGUE WITH God

Contrary Action

Chapter 28
- ## I Was Born To Sing.
  ## Overcoming My Own Fear

"Obstaculum es difficilis locus vos animadverto ut vos take vestri eyes off calx."

"Obstacles are the difficult situations you see when you take your eyes off the goal."

Mark Twain

I will share with you my own personal experience with overcoming fear. When I was a little girl I loved to sing. I would come home from school and sit on the floor in front of my record player and sing along to music for hours and hours. I would get lost in the music. I wanted to be a singer when I grew up. I dreamed of being on stage and everyone loving me. I wanted to be a star. But I had one "slight" problem. I was terrified to sing in front of people. No, not just terrified. I was horrified and paralyzed with fear. In fact, I was afraid to be singled out and put in front of people in any way, at any time.

I am black and white and grew up in the 60's, 70's and 80's at a time when being black was still being criticized by some people. I grew up in a very Italian community and many were racist, so I was made me the butt of endless cruel racial comments. Comments I am glad most black or bi-racial children today don't have to deal with. My childhood was very difficult for me in terms of being afraid of what people thought about me. I was very scarred by the experience and terrified of rejection. I was experiencing rejection every day and it hurt. Avoiding it became very important to me.

I remember being at Sea World with my mom and brother and they called for a volunteer from the audience to come on stage. I literally felt sick to my stomach, turned white and shrank in my seat, for fear they might call on me. I had stage fright so badly I cried whenever I was called on for anything at school. I would literally freeze in fear.

All that being said, now the question was: how was I going to become a singer? How could I stand on stage and sing in front of people who will judge me? there was no way, so how the heck was I going to pursue my dream?

As the years went by, my desire to sing grew stronger inside me. Singing was all I could think about. As I grew up through Junior High and High School, I would come home everyday and sing for five or six hours into a tape recorder with my records as backing music. I pretended I was singing on the records. Sometimes when I was at a store shopping, I would sing out loud without noticing it and someone would comment on how beautiful my voice was and ask me to sing for them. I would immediately shut my mouth, make some excuse and get away from them as quickly as I could.

When I was 19 or 20 years old I decided I was going to get over my fear of singing no matter what it took. I made a conscious decision, a conscious choice, to force myself to walk through this paralyzing fear. It took many, many steps, many years and many conscious choices of walking through the fear. These choices were difficult, scary and often painful but they were worth it!

First, I started to sing in one of those Kareoke booths in the mall. I got to feel like a recording artist in there and the only person I had to sing in front of was the engineer who taped me. He always commented on how great I sounded, so I got used to singing in front of him. Then a year later he invited me to sing in a talent show he was putting on which in addition to others, would all the best singers who recorded in his Kareoke recording booth. I was terrified but I said yes.

It was a huge event with over 500 people in the audience. The Mayor of New Haven, Connecticut Biagio DiLieto was the event's MC. I remember sitting backstage before it was my turn on a bench with my head between my legs ready to die. Mayor DiLieto was sitting next to patting me on the back saying, "don't worry kid everything is going to be alright." Thank God for him. I didn't win the contest that night but I beat my fear. I was so proud of myself.

After the show, it was one of the happiest and most encouraging moments of my life. My Dad came up to me and said proudly, "Wendy, looks like you might belong up there on stage." Hearing that my Dad thought I belonged up there that meant the world to me. Then walking down the street to our car to leave, I saw a few women point to me, saying: "Oooh! she was good too. Yeah, she was." I have to tell you that night felt good. I felt so encouraged. I was beaming.

The next step I took was to enroll in a voice class. I was attending Southern Connecticut State University as a Psycholgoy Major so I joined a beginners singing class. Suddenly I was required to sing every week in front of 15 or 20 students. Each week I had to prepare 2 songs to sing and then the entire class critiqued me in writing and handed it to me! It was terrifying. It certainly didn't hurt that every critique was favorable. I spent 1 year studying voice at SCSU. Wanting to expand my training, I went to the Yale campus to meet with a group of Yale University Music Grad students who taught voice. After I sang for them in an audition, they looked at each other, then at me and said, " I don't see what we can teach you. You're great!"

Encouraged by these experiences, I packed my bags and moved to Los Angeles to become a star. Within months I met a record producer, made a demo, did backing vocals for a group on Capital records and was in 2 music videos. Each time I felt the sickness in my stomach, the agony of my fear, but I forced myself to do it anyways. I pushed through it. I heard fearful thoughts in my head the whole time I was doing something. Some moments they subsided but only for a minute. With each new situation, I was completely terrified. However I made a decision, a conscious choice, that I was NOT going to let fear stop me or hold me back in my life no matter what.

My journey through fear continued. Next someone introduced me to Rene Van Verseveld, a famous Dutch record producer who had many hit records throughout Europe and was looking for singers to work with. He liked my voice so he flew me to Holland, Europe, where I worked with him for four years singing and song writing.

I remember the first time Ronald van Der Meijden an A&R guy from CNR Records came to the studio to listen to finished tracks we had done. I hid by myself on the other side of the building terrified, afraid to come out and face anyone. They were a group of record people judging me and it felt horrible. I went through hours of fear sitting on the other side of the building with my head between my legs or pacing back and forth, wondering why I was even doing this. What if they hated it? Maybe they would like it. I hoped they did. turned out they loved it and signed me to a Record Deal

The first three records I made became top 30 hits in various European countries. They were played on television shows and in movies. I even heard them on the radio at gas stations when I pumped my gas. One day I was at a country club swimming pool changing in the locker room and I heard a little girl in the next row singing one of my songs. How thrilling that was!

I went on to shoot two music videos in Amsterdam and each time I went in front of the camera I was fearful, terrified, and exhilerated at the same time. However I felt I belonged in front of the camera.

I remember sitting backstage in Paris at the French-MTV Television Studios getting ready to perform live for thousands of people. I was nervous, but excited. I had been taking Contrary Action for a few years now so I was starting to see and feel the results of it. I wasn't scared to death back stage anymore. I was excited more than anything. When I finally hit the stage I felt great, I connected with the audience. They loved me and gave me great feedback. I was starting to get used to singing in front of people so it was not as scary for me anymore.

My music videos played on MTV, VH1 and BET and I performed through many European countries. The record label flew me and my group back to America to promote one of the records, specifically, we were to be an awards presenter at a big music show. I was in my element, many of my idols were there. I was one of the performers at this event and when I got on stage that night I felt NO fear.

Do you hear me? I felt NO fear. I felt high. I felt ecstatic. I felt Joy. I felt ready to do my best and give it all I got. I felt on top of the world, and finally I was free. Free to go out there and sing my heart out with nothing holding me back. I had done it.

I can tell you that was one of the happiest moments of my life. The freedom to be myself, the freedom to be who I am without fear of other people's opinions or negative voices in my head. I had overcome my own fear.

My music was being used in television commercials, tv shows and films. I was teaching voice privately in Holland, had many students throughout the years I was there and loved sharing my experience and resources with other people who dreamed of becoming singers.

When I moved back to Los Angeles, I wanted to learn everything about the entertainment industry so for 5 years I wore many hats: I was an assistant in several talent agencies and management companies representing huge stars. I worked for the legendary publicist Lee Solters at his top PR firm, and worked in music licensing at Virgin Records. I did extra work in films and tv, co produced a music video and worked on the Sony Studio lot assisting a famous Director. I worked my through the "University of Hollywood" until I became a Music Booking Agent and finally a Talent Agent representing many well known stars. I attended the Grammy parties, the big award shows, and I loved living the Hollywood life.

As a Singer, I had reached some level of commercial success back in Europe, but I was starting from scratch back here in the States.

I had a new fear I wanted to overcome. I had never sung with a live band. All my records previously were dance music where I had dancers around me, headsets, fast music and an audience of young people dancing and screaming. So I became the lead singer of the 7-piece Blues and R&B Band "Billy's Night Out" and delved into a completely different arena. After my day job, we were playing evenings in clubs where people were sitting still watching me sing and I had to really entertain them. Just me. Now it was all about my voice, my stage presence and my performance. I dreamed of doing this all my life and in my heart I wanted to be great at this.

After two years with this band, I reached a level of performing on stage that was exceptional. I mean I was on fire. I loved performing and I was very good at it. Deep down inside, underneath all the mean comments from others in my youth, I always knew I would be. I always knew I was shaped for this. The mistake I had made when I was younger was that a part of me had listened to the mean comments and I believed their words. <u>Always be careful with your words. They are very easy to let out and impossible to take back.</u>

I got an agent, opened for the Four Tops, sang at the John Anson Ford Theatre in Los Angeles, made a record with Solomon Burke and Little Richard, and on sang for four Verizon commercials. I had another dance song on the radio and I performed at big Hollywood charity events with Gregory Hines, Nell Carter, Raquel Welch and Edward James Olmos. I sang in Beverly Hills at the Bizantine Royal Ball for Kings, Queens and other members of royalty from all over the world. I sang back up for Wayne Brady and Billie Meyers. I recorded with Candy Dulfer and sang with Johnny Lang at a Grammy Party.

I had so much fun doing all of these performances and I was very proud of myself for how far I had come. I was no longer a scared little girl dreaming of being a singer. I had actually become a professional singer and was very good at it.

At this time I had written quite a few songs for myself and others. My voice appeared on over 60 records and

I was putting the finishing touches on my 3rd solo CD. In a few years, I would be opening WAW Talent Training and Performance Studios in southern California and bringing all of my years of experience and knowledge of the entertainment industry to newcomers with big dreams.

But back then, another hurdle was yet to come for me. Even after all that time performing, sometimes in front of thousands of people, I was still afraid to sing in front of my family or friends in the living room. For years my mother would introduce me to people and say, "this is my daughter Wendy, she is a singer and you have to hear her voice...Wendy sing something." And I would freeze completely, always turn her down and make some excuse, apologizing to her friends. I was too afraid too stand there and sing for 5 or 6 friends or family. Interesting right? Well you know my relationship with fear and Contrary Action. I was determined to get over that too, so I forced myself finally to do it on various occasions when my mother asked. That got easier eventually, too.

Then came my Grandmother's 100th Birthday party and family Reunion. My entire family was there about 150 people. My Aunt Ginny asked me to sing for everyone. That panic and fear hit my stomach again like a ton of bricks. I told her no and was very busy in my head making up all kinds of reasons why I couldn't possibly do it. My beautiful aunt looked me straight in the eyes and said: "Wendy have I ever asked you for anything?"

Her comment hit me very deeply. No she never had. It must have been very important to her for her to ask me. So I decided to get over my fear at that moment and just do it. I told her "yes of course," and made myself get up and sing in front of my entire family; cousins, aunts, uncles and all. Oh my God! I walked to the front of the room where my little Grandmother was sitting. She hardly recognized any of us the sweet thing. I sang happy birthday to her. Then I sang "We are family" to my family and then I sang "Amazing Grace" for them, because that is what I was given that day.

I came back to my table and there were tears flowing from my brother's eyes and that was worth everything to me - my whole journey - for I had touched his heart, and it was a moment I will never forget.

I tell you this story to help you realize you can overcome any fear you have - if you choose to. <u>Fear will always be in your life, that will never change, but your relationship to fear must change.</u> To overcome fear all you have to do is make a decision to overcome your fear and walk through it. Yes, it will be difficult and scary, but when you choose to walk through it, the universe will conspire to help you fulfill your purpose. Oprah Winfrey once said "We are each here with a purpose. As soon as you start honoring your calling, the entire universe will step up to help you because that is why you are here."

After my family reunion, I finally had the courage to record my 1st Solo CD entitled "As I Am." which was many years coming. It was dream for me, a dream I had since childhood, and I am proud to say I finally have accomplished it.

Know this, God will always provide opportunities for you to take. It's your job to take them. Because I am strong practicer of Contrary Action, I was willing to face my fears and take Contrary Actions, which have changed my life for the better, over and over again.

When opportunities present themselves to you, take advantage of them! It will be a journey well worth travelling. It will not always be easy, but learning to be okay with yourself, being who you really are, and sharing all the gifts and talents God gave you is what life is all about.

You can visit the website of my school WAW Talent Training and Performance Studios at www.WAWentertainment.com

PART TWO

MY DIALOGUE WITH God

Contrary Action

Chapter 29
- Overcoming Selfishness

"Don't reputo minor of vestri. Recordor vestri minor sepius."

"Don't think less of yourself. Think of yourself less often."

Wendy Wright

One of life's purposes is to overcome Selfishness. Selfishness is like a plague that all human beings are born with. It is like a disease that is contagious. It is the root of all problems, all pain and suffering. Whenever we feel emotional pain it is because we are being selfish. Whenever we feel peace it is because we are being selfless or "self-less." Recently, I had a realization about my father who came to visit. I hadn't seen him in a few-years. We live on opposite coasts, yet we talked every few days. This trip he came to visit me and spent two weeks here in California with my brother and I. When he got here the bronchitis he had just gotten over back home started to reoccur and he was sick two days after his arrival with us. He was having difficulty breathing, we took him to the urgent care facility where he got all the treatment and medicine he needed. Needless to say his visit was one where he needed to take it easy.

He spent five days with me and then five days with my brother and returned home. It was great to see him and although I am a grown woman, I still has some expectations of what I wanted from him: A little more attention, a little more time. However, while he was here he took a few walks by himself, preferred to wait at the pharmacy alone rather than have breakfast with us and I made some judgements about his behavior. I didn't say anything to him, just quietly thought him selfish. He came all the way out here and he was still all about himself. It triggered memories of all the times he chose to write over being with is family.

Well it took two months after he had gone for me to realize I had been the one who was selfish. My daily prayers to God ashking Him to remove my selfishness were paying off. I rembered my Dad was sick during his visit, I was still feeling like the 11-year old girl who just couldn't get enough of my daddy. I was not being compasionate, nor did I take into consideration how bad we feel when we are sick! He could hardly even breathe sometimes. I needed to give him understanding not judgement. Maybe he was more comfortable waiting at the drug store and not cramped in a booth at the restaurant. Maybe he felt better when he was walking and getting fresh air. The point is... it was not about me. But with us human being it always about us. It is always about me, about you. We are selfish.

I called and apologized to him for being selfish and demanding. Today I am consciously choosing to love him just the way he is and stop any and all expectations. It's a process. We are always unpeeling the layers of selfishness within us.

Most of us aren't even aware of our selfishness and the degree to which it infects our lives and relationships. If you look at your own personal relationships with your family, parents, siblings, children, co workers....isn't it always all about you? They don't do things the way I want them to. They don't Love me the way I want them to. They aren't listening to me. They don't do this or that "right." If only they would just do things the way I think they should. We find all kinds of reasons to justify our selfishness.

It's like you were given the only book about how life should work and nobody else got a copy, right? If only they had your book and did things your way then everything would be okay. Look at the arguments you have with people in your life. They are usually about you getting offended in some way when people don't meet your expectations. Right? If you start looking at this closely you will see that it is always all about you.

The greatest downfalls of humanity is selfishness, self-centeredness and self-seeking. These are the way in which we fail as human beings and fall short of God's higher purpose for our lives. Human selfishness is the most destructive force in nature, more destructive than an earthquake, a hurricane, a flood, even disease. Human selfishness is at the root of pain and suffering. We have the power to choose between love and fear, good and evil, war and peace. We are faced with these decisions every day. When we choose selfishness over self-lessness we have poverty, hunger, hate, racism, child abuse, rape, murder, wars and disease and starvation in most of the world. If we chose Love, and if we were all acting like Christ imagine, what state the world would be in. John Lennon addressed this in his song "Imagine." The words to his song strike a chord of truth deep within us. This can be a world where people live as one, lovingly.

How does that come about? The solution is called choice. Choice is the most powerful quality we human beings have. We can choose to be loving and deny fear at any time. However, first we must become conscious that we even possess this ability called choice. People are not even conscious that they have that choice. They feel they are who they are because of their circumstances, their history, their parents, their culture, their countries, their religion, their race, their gender. They have many reasons they think they are not in control of who they are, yet this is completely untrue.

We human beings have the power to transcend all the negative factors of our lives and still choose love, hope, light, peace, health, happiness, tolerance, kindness and forgiveness of ourselves and the whole of humanity. Viktor Frankl discusses these principals in his book, "Man's Search for Meaning." His book is about a man in a Nazi war camp who comes to believe that people can take away everything – his family, his freedom, everything - except they could not take away the way he chose to respond to what they did to him. Frankl said, "The last of one's freedoms is to choose one's attitude in any given circumstance."

Change on the planet starts with one's own personal journey into consciousness. You cannot change the entire planet, but you can change yourself. As the honorable Mohatmas Ghandi said, "Be the change you wish to see in the world." You can choose to change how you think, act, and react. You can choose how you behave and treat others. You can decide to be loving in the face of ALL things. The answer to peace on Earth lies within you.

God's greatest gift to you is the power to choose. You must exercise this power to strengthen it. Each time you choose love over fear you become stronger. You must make it your personal mission to stop being a victim of your circumstances, your childhood, your unattained goals, your broken heart or your loss of faith in humanity. No more excuses for why YOU are not loving, for why you are not being your best or being all you can be. You are the cause of all of your choices. You and only you. You must realize you can make a difference in yourself and the world around you.

You have the power to touch the lives of everyone you come in contact with. You can help and inspire everyone around you. One light can shine and inspire many people. And the more people who shine the light of love from their hearts, the brighter the world will become.

If you choose to follow Christ, the Buddha of any other Master Teacher don't get bogged down and distracted by their religious doctrines. Stay focused on the words and works of these great teachers. Focus on their qualities. snd their actions. Study how they treated people and themselves. You can ask God directly to help you be more like Christ, the Buddha, Ghandi, Martin Luther King, Mother Theresa or anyone else who has developed the ability to sacrifice themselves for the sake of others. Ask Him to help you be more loving, patient, kind, gentle and unconditionally loving.

Selfishness is a disease each person has and it is up to each person to cure themselves of this disease with God's help. No one else can do it for us. The first step to recover from Selfishness is awareness. Becoming aware. I remember first becoming aware of my selfishness about five years ago. Someone recommended I hit my knees in the morning and pray: " God I am selfish, please remove this defect of character. I don't want to be this way anymore."

I started doing that everyday. I did it for a year straight everyday. I did not understand, nor can I explain the magic of prayer, but it worked. I started seeing places where I was selfish that I hadn't even noticed before. First simple things, then more complex manifestations.

The simple ones were ridiculous. One day after I had finished eating at a fast food restaurant, I got up to throw my trash away to be considerate of those around me and help to keep the place clean. Not selfish right? Well, I get to the trash can and there is a guy there changing the bag. I impatiently try to find a way to throw my trash in while he is trying to change it and all of a sudden it dawns on me that this man is trying to do his job and I am being selfish!!! I immediately apologized to him and waited for him to finish changing the bag. But you see, for just a minute it was all about me again. It is always about me and about you.

That is why we get so angry when people cut in front of us on the road, or get served before us in line, or get to go to an open register when we were waiting there longer-because it is always about us. We are afraid that if we give to others there won't be enough for ourselves. If we give up our space in line somehow we will miss out. But miss out on what? If we let people go in front of us they win. They win what? We are all so petty and infested with selfishness we miss so many opportunities to Love, to give Love and to be of service to others. We have the mentality of lack: If I give them mine there won't be enough for me. If I let them in they will be better than me. Do you notice how these thoughts are all about ourselves?

They say "money is the root of all evil." I disagree. Selfishness is the root of all "evil". We must become conscious of this sickness within ourselves and work diligently to remove it. That is the only way we will find healing in our relationships and in the world.

Contrary Actions:

1) Do something nice for someone else without letting them know, or telling anyone else about it. If anyone else knows, it doesn't count.

2) Get on your knees everyday for 1 year and pray: "God I am selfish and self-centered. Please remove this defect of character from me. I don't want to be this way any more."

3) Be of service to others, not a doormat. (There is a difference) Offer help, try to notice other people and see what you can contribute to other people's lives.

In other words GIVE more, TAKE less.

PART TWO

MY DIALOGUE WITH God

Contrary Action

Chapter 30
-    Life's Not Fair

"Vita est patientia." Illic est patientia , illic est a causa pro patientia , illic est an terminus of patientia , quod illic est a semita of meditor ut puts an terminus ut patientia."

"Life is suffering." There is suffering, there is a cause for suffering, there is an end of suffering, and there is a path of practice that puts an end to suffering."

Buddah, Four Noble Truths

L ife's not really fair. We struggle with that reality, but it's true. Some people have healthy babies, some people have babies with severe birth defects or babies that are stillborn. Some people's parents live to a ripe old age, while other people's parents die relatively young. Some children are born into healthy, happy homes where they are Loved and others are born into homes where they are sexually abused or physically beaten. Some people die of starvation while others are dining in 4-star restaurants. Some people die of illness in parts of the world with poor medical care, while in other parts of the world those illnesses are very treatable.

Life's not really fair. But we all have to learn to deal with that. When life seems unfair, your attitude can make all the differnce. The old saying applies here: "When life gives you lemons, make lemonade." It's simple, yet true.

Put another way, by Wayne Dyer who said, "If I could define enlightenment briefly I would say it is "the quiet acceptance of what is." How we react to life will determine the amount of happiness and joy we experience in our lives. We can either take our hits as they come and keep our eyes on all we have to be grateful for, or focus on the injustices and become embittered and angry. There may be hidden meaning in the disappointments of life. If you remember that Universe is compassionate and wise you will be open to learning from all experiences.

Conscious living requires we become conscious of how we are thinking and reacting to life. Conscious of the choices we make and the actions we take. It is well within our realm of power to wake up every day and be grateful for all that is going well in our lives. To be as loving as we can be to ourselves, as well as others. To try to give something back to the world and become a positive light in our communities. The alternative is to sit at home feeling slighted by our "lot in life and isolate in a world of self-pity and sadness.

Let me give you a perfect example. Susie was born into a middle class family in Southern California. Her mother was a teacher and her father was a white collar worker. Susie's father was inept at having personal relationships and intimacy so he never formed a loving bond with his daughter. They didn't do things together and he never expressed Love or interest in her. As she grew up the pain of her situation ate a hole in her heart that grew larger year after year.

As she struggled to get some Love from her father she was denied it at every attempt. Susie learned to withdraw emotionally and to withdraw physically from others.

She did not have the intention to make somethingout of her life, to a difference, perhaps go give Love, time and attention to other desperate children who grew up like she did. Instead Susie withdrew into her own private hell of depression, pills, isolation and tremendous weight gain. Further, she had no ability to have a healthy marital relationship.

She eventually got married, but refused to have sex with her husband. She had a college degree but didn't work for 15 years She gave up her passion for art. She simply gave nothing to the world and sat around feeling sorry for herself because the "lot in life" she was given was unacceptable to her. She gave up her personal power because life "wasn't fair." She then made choices that made her life even more unhappy emotionally, spiritually, physically, and sexually. She estranged relationships with friends, no activities she enjoyed, did no charity work and became useless, instead of a useful person in society.

Her attitude kept her stuck in life. Instead of becoming a powerful woman for example; a champion of children's rights, or perhap a founder of a children's medical center in the inner city, she simply felt sorry for herself.

How we deal with and choose to respond to our "lot in life" and the unfair elements of it, determines the level of happiness, joy and usefulness we create. It will take a willingness on the part of Susie to turn her life around. The problem is people get so attached to their victim role and blaming others for their plot in life, they have a hard time accepting personal responsibility for the misery they have created in their own lives. Yes, Susie's father was a lousy parent. But did the worse in him have to determine who Susie would be the rest of her life? Did Susie have to limit herself to being defined by this one man?

Becoming "conscious" of our actions and reactions gives us the power to change them and ultimately our reality. Instead of stewing in self pity and resentment, Susie could have chosen to do whatever it took to change her life to one worth living. She could have contribute her talents and efforts to help others and could have realized she was better off than many of the other people in the world.

She could have forgiven her father and realized that he did and had done the best he can. I use this analogy. Her dad had 5 cents in his pocket. Susie wanted a dollar. He gave her the five cents in his pocket, everything he had. It wasn't the dollar she wanted and maybe even longed for and needed, but it was all he had, and he gave it to her. People do the best they can with what they have. They can't give something they haven't got. How you deal with that reality is completely up to you.

There are people who were born into the worst situations of life and are still determined to make the best out of life. I am inspired by people like theoretical physicist Steven Hawking, who suffers from motor neurone diseas (otherwise known as ALS or Lou Gehrig's Disease) which has left him almost completely paralyzed and the international motivational speaker and author Nick Vujicic who was born with out limbs and penned the book "Life Without Limits." These men have made powerful choices to succeed in life, in the face of major challenges.

We have the power to choose. God gave that to us as another way to even the playing field against unfairness. When life seems unfair we can take responsibility. Don't be a victim. Change your outlook. Pain is just a part of our spiritual growth. Have you noticed we learn a lot from pain? Often our biggest lessons are learned through pain. Pain may be God's loudest wake up call, since we are so good at ignoring his gentle, daily persuasions.

Here are a couple of stories to consider about two different men:

When Paul was a child he sexually abused at knifepoint by a couple that ran a daycare center. This couple sexually abused and raped all the children in the day care with knives to their throats. Today, he runs a successful computersoftware company and is a generous and kind person. Although Paul has some intimacy issues, he has worked through much of the wreckage of his childhood and is determined to have the life he is worthy of having. He gets up every day trying to be his best and to achieve his goals and dreams, helping everyone he can along the way.

Now let's look at Steve. He was beaten bloody in the crib by his mother as an infant. In his forties now, Steve still has personal scarring that prevents him from having successful relationships with women. His fear of intimacy is so great, he is constantly suspicious of the activities of the women he gets involved with. He tries to control everything they say and do, what they wear, who their friends are, how they speak, is verbally abusive all the time and physically abusive some of the time. He has never dealt with his past and how it's affected his present. He hasn't accepted the "unfairness of his lot in life," and has remained a victim throughout his life and feels sorry for himself. He blames women, fears women, and keeps creating and recreating circumstances in which he isn't Loved. When these things are pointed out to him he blames the other person Steve may never become conscious of these truths.

The challenge for Paul and Steve is the willingness to see the truth and to accept their lot in life. Unfair as it was they can still become the best human beings they can. We can either be a victim to the misdeeds of others for the duration of our lives, or we can become strong powerful creators of a life worth living. The choice is ours. Choice is one of our greatest God given gifts.

The research and spiritual journey I have been on for the past 30 years has taught me many things.

1.   We are here to become the best versions of ourselves that we can be.

2.   We are here to make a positive difference in the lives of others.

3.   We cannot fix other people.

4.   Our own choices can lead us into misery or joy.

5.   People will take us down with them, if we let them.

6.   We teach other people how to treat us by what we allow them to do to us.

7.   That we have a lot to be grateful for and an attitude of gratitude makes all the difference between happiness and self-pity.

8.   We may not have been given the Love we required, desired or deserved, but we have plenty of Love inside us to give to others who require, desire and

deserve it.

9. There are so many places in our own communities where we can lend our time, our hearts, our minds, gifts, talks, and abilities, and be a blessing to the world and not waste our lives pining away for what could have been or should have been if only life was fair.

10. If we wake up in the morning and look life squarely in the eye, ask God how we can best serve Him, ourselves, and the people around us and live our lives as if only He is watching, then we can create wonderful, useful lives that bring us and countless others pleasure and joy.

Being a person who lives "consciously" means:

1. Being honest with ourselves about ourselves.

2. No longer blaming others.

3. Taking actions that will take our lives in the direction we really desire to go, even if it means we are afraid.

4. Being willing to admit we're wrong.

5.   Being willing to stop and try something new if what we're doing isn't working.

6.   Surrounding ourselves with healthy positive people who see the best in us and want the best for us.

7.   Getting rid of toxic people and toxic relationships.

I always say, think of your life as a play. You are on stage and you have the front rows, mid-section, and balcony areas to the side. The front rows are reserved. Don't invite anyone in your front row who isn't your biggest fan. In dating, in marriage, in friendship, in work, those seats are reserved for people who Love you, care for you and are there to give you a standing ovation. Anyone in those seats heckling you, hurting you, abusing you, verbally, physically, psychologically, emotionally, spiritually, financially or in anyway, cannot sit in the front seats of your life. In fact, if I were you I would have an usher escort them out of the theater altogether. However, sometimes quite unfortunately, those people are members of your own family, so you may just have to have security escort them to a far away section of the theater where you can't hear or see them. People who abuse you do not get access to you,

Often our worst enemies exist right in our own families and how do we deal with that? By not allowing ourselves to be affected by the things they do or say. This is very hard to do when it is your primary family: mother, father, brothers, sisters, aunts or uncles. But we have to remember that even though they were born into our space and family, they are not automatically entitled to front row seats. If we have identified them as hecklers, and since we can't change anyone else but ourselves, we have to learn to move them out of our way.

No, life is not always fair. Some of us are born with family members who have abused every priviledge of being close to us. Some of us are born with fewer limbs, or no eyesight, or have experienced the loss of loved ones at an unaccpetable age, from unnaceptable circumstances. And yes, we can choose to be bitter and suffer for the remainder of our own lives, or we can choose to accept that life is not fair, and that we can choose to be happy in spite of it.

It's hard to do, but that's our challenge. How do we do that? With an Attitiude of Gratitude.

PART TWO

MY DIALOGUE WITH God

Contrary Action

Chapter 31
- ## An Attitude of Gratitude

Operor quis vos can, per quis vos have, qua vos es.

"Do what you can, with what you have, where you are."

Theodore Roosevelt

While writing this book, I spoke to a man who told me that his wife was jealous of a couple they knew who had a multi-million dollar house in Pasadena. He was very upset that his wife feeling this way because this man was right in the middle of building her a $900,000 house from the ground up with his bare hands. He had personally designed this house for her and was building it for her as a gift. I saw the pain in his eyes and was saddened by her lack of gratitude and appreciation for her husband. Jealousy and greed blinds us so often to all the gifts we do have. A lack of gratitude divides and separates people, putting them in an unhealthy competition with others. He has a Porsche and I don't. They have more money than I do. They have more friends than we do. He or she is dressed better than I am. Why do they get to travel so much? And on and on....We focus on what we don't have, rather than what we DO have. That's a big mistake.

God put each of us in our own race. We are in our own lane in the journey to God. God arranges all that we need to finish that race and reach Him. He gives us different spiritual gifts, talents, goals and obstacles. Our job is not to spend time looking at other people's lanes and wishing we had what they had. Our job is to focus on our own race and be grateful for what God has given us.

I believe having an attitude of gratitude can make all the difference in life between being happy or not. If you wake up in the morning thinking about all you don't have and all that others have you are going to get up on the wrong side of the bed. On the other hand, if you spend a moment before rising, reflecting in your mind, making a mental list of all you have to be grateful for, you will get out of bed with a smile in your heart and an attitude of gratitude that you will carry with you happily through the day. But don't take my word for it. Try it...

Want an emotional pick-me-up right now? Take five minutes right now and make a Gratitude list. Write down everything you have to be grateful for. Walk around your house and write things down; a dishwasher, microwave, a bed to sleep in, hot running water, electricity, refrigerator full of food, your eyesight. List everything you can think of that is good in your life.

Done? Now that you're all done how do you feel? It is hard to feel bad when you have an attitude of gratitude, when you are focusing on all the good in your life. Post this list where you can read it often and add to it as you think of new things.

I make gratitude lists often sometimes mentally when I am driving and sometimes when I really need to get a correct perspective of my life. I believe you determine your own level of happiness by how conscious you are of all you have to be grateful for. Abraham Lincoln said "Most people are as happy as they make up their minds to be."

Take a moment and consider the following: It is a very interesting way to look at our lives, and so true: If the Earth's population was shrunk into a village of just 100 people, with all the human ratios existing in the world still remaining, what would this tiny diverse village look lie? That's exactly what Phillip M. Harter, a medical doctor at the Stanford University School of Medicine, attempted to figure out.

This is what he found:

57	would be Asian
21	would be European
14	would be from the Western Hemi sphere
8	would be African
52	would be female
48	would be male
70	would be non-Christian
30	would be Christian
89	would be heterosexual
11	would be homosexual

6	people would possess 59% of the entire world's wealth, and all 6 would be from the United States
80	would live in substandard housing
70	would be unable to read
50	would suffer from malnutrition
1	would be near death
1	would be pregnant
1	would have a college education
1	would own a computer

The following is an anonymous interpretation. Think of it this way. If you live in a good home, have plenty to eat and can read, you are a member of a very select group. And if you have a good house, food, can read and have a computer, you are among the very elite. If you woke up this morning with more health than illness, .you are more fortunate than the millions who will not survive this week.

If you have never experienced the danger of battle, the loneliness of imprisonment, the agony of torture, or the pangs of starvation, you are ahead of 500 million people in the world.

If you can attend a church meeting without fear of harassment, arrest, torture or death, you are more fortunate than 3 billion people in the world can't. If you have food in the refrigerator, clothes on your back, a roof over-head and a place to sleep, you are richer than 75% of the people in this world.

If you have money in the bank, in your wallet, and spare change in a dish someplace, you are among the top 8% of the world's wealthy. If your parents are still alive and married, you are very rare, even in the United States. If you hold your head with a smile on your face and are truly thankful, you are blessed because the majority can, but most do not.

If you can hold someone's hand, hug them or even touch them on the shoulder you are blessed, because you can offer a healing touch. If you can read this message, you more blessed than over 2 billion people in the world that cannot read.

So have a good day, and count your blessings!

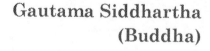

3

III

CONTRARY ACTION - PART THREE

OUR RELATIONSHIP WITH OTHERS

"Evinco oneself est a maioribus negotium quam victum alius."

"To conquer oneself is a greater task than conquering others."

Gautama Siddhartha (Buddha)

PART THREE

MY DIALOGUE WITH God

Contrary Action

Chapter 32
- ## You Can't Control Other People

"Panton vos es obviam macero vos. Panton vos es pro empowers vos."

"Everything you are against weakens you. Everything you are for empowers you."

Wayne Dyer

This is a very important chapter. The biggest source of pain in our lives is often our relationships with other people. We are all hurt deeply at one time or another by other people. We all look so hard for people to be the answer to our happiness rather than God. I finally came to the point of being in so much pain by my own actions and the actions of others around me, that I did the appropriate work on myself that led to the solutions and answers for myself. I finally live the life that I had been seeking for years: I have relationships that work.

Prior to this change in awareness that took place in me during the many years I wrote this book in daily prayer and meditation with God, I was hoping my relationships would be the source of all my happiness. But I have realized, that the source of our happiness doesn't reside outside of ourselves, it resides within us. People will not meet your expectations, they simply won't. People are flawed and will always let you down sometimes, even when they love you. You cannot find your happiness in other people, only in God. Put God first and everything else must follow.

My father always said, "Wendy, the hardest thing you will ever do in life is relationships." Makes sense. We all have problems with relationships. The 10 commandments are directives for how to have relationships, that's how much help we need with them! Problems in relationships most often happen because there is a power struggle. People are trying to control each other and neither wants to give up their position of being right. Instead, they want the OTHER person to change what they are doing.

Often people have a hard time leaving allowing other people to do things their own way. People try to play God. We want everybody around us to act and think like we think they should. We get upset when they don't behave, think, and speak the way we think they should. Perhaps you can relate to that. Some people try to control others passively, they are called passive-aggressives. They are polite and manipulative, They don't let you know they are upset, they just quietly pull away their attention to try and manipulate you with their silence or non-agressive behaviors.

People's overtly aggressive methods to control others are too many too count but include: burning people at the stake, crucifying people on the cross, murder, rape, domestic violence, war, and on and on.

But think about this, in your own body your heart is beating and you have no control over that. You are breathing in and out and you have no control over that. Your body is digesting and eliminating food and you have no control over that either. Thoughts are constantly racing through your mind as you compare and analyze everything, criticize and critique yourself, the world and everybody in it. These voices never seem to shut up. Are you in charge of these thoughts? There is so much going on in your OWN body that you have no control over, how could you possibly have control over what is happening in another person's body or mind?

Often in our personal relationsips, we go to any lengths to get people to do what we want them to do. We have an Illusion of Control Here is a rule of thumb, an easy way to see if you are trying to control someone in your life. If you say something to someone once, you are simply stating an opinion or making a suggestion. If you say it more than once, you are trying to control them.

Once you have said something the second time you are trying to sway them to your way of thinking; trying to change their mind or actions and trying to manipulate them to see or do something differently. You can't change people. Any attempt at this will end in futility and a lot of wasted time! Your time and your life is precious, you need to honor that.

When you criticize, correct, or try to control people you are in fact saying they are not okay the way they are.

You are also saying you will not Love them, approve of them or often act lovingly towards them until they do things your way. And believe me they do the same thing to you. We all do this to each other, and it is NOT UNCONDITIONAL LOVE. Sadly, the Love we give is often very conditional.

Criticizing, correcting and trying to control people are fast ways to undermine and sabotage your relationships with family, friends, co-workers or Lovers. It damages other people's self esteem and they end up resenting you for that. People who criticize, correct and control are not fun to be around. No one likes to be around someone who acts like the punisher everytime they do something differthan they would. And that is exactly what it is; simply different. We all have our different ways of doing things. In fact there are a great many ways of doing the same thing and getting good results. That is the beauty of being created in Gods image, we are creative beings and we are inventive. So when someone has invented a way of doing things other than your own "perfect way," remember to honor the God in them and let people be who they are. Your relationships will improve 10-fold.

Giving up this pattern of control is going to be difficult because as human being we are very attached to being "right" and getting their way

We all have to let go of the illusion that we have power over other people. We never have power over anybody else. Not their feelings, their actions, their thinking or their behavior. In the recovery movement I learned about the 3 C's: I didn't cause it, I can't control it and I can't cure it. This saying helped me realize I was absolutely not responsible for who people were, never have been, and never would be.

The moment I became aware of this and accepted it, my life immediately began to change. I felt a sigh of relief knowing I didn't have to fight anyone or anything anymore. That people are going to be whoever they are no matter what I do and I could just accept that fact. That let me off the hook and I began to experience a peace and understanding I had never known.

I know a couple that fight every day. They are constantly criticizing the other and speaking badly about eachother to people outside of their relationship. They argue about the actions the other takes, or doesn't take. They contantly try to force their opions on eachother. Neither one of them are listening to how the other feels. I wonderf if they even care. I have suggested counseling to them for years, but they are both commiteed to being right and neither one of them wants the other one to be right about anything. Year after year, they are destroying the intimacy and the bond they once shared. Sadly, neither one of them are willing to do anything about it. They would rather be right than happy.

To have peace in our lives we must realize that we are powerless over other people, places and things. We have to learn to accept people and situations the way they are.

People may not change, but we can set boundaries about what we will and will not accept from them. We can remove ourseleves from situations or people when it's dangerous for us. But we have to choose our battles. Most things we should just let go of.

The saying, "Maybe you are right" is a very powerful tool. Use sometime. If you are in an argument with someone. Stop defending your position and just say, "Maybe you are right."This statement doesn't say you agree or disagree with them, it also doesn't hurt them or cause a conflict to escalate. It simply puts an end to the argument. Try it sometime.

The situation often difuses instantly. Do you want to have peace or war? Anger and stress are unhealthy and can lead to illness. It's not worth it. When we let go of our expectations and demands upon others, we experience more peace and health. It is transforming.

Our reactions to other people is what cause us pain. When we learn not to react and just let things be exactly what they are we exerience more peace inside ourselevs. What you resist will persist.

It takes work to live a conscious life, to become aware of your limitations, to allow others to be who they are without trying to control their lives, and to learn to react to people in new and different ways. It takes work to unlearn old thinking and old behaviors and apply new ones. It takes a little change at a time, one day at a time, aand you end up with an extraordinary life you are proud to live.

I pray all the time for God to remove every single thing I do that stands between me and my faithfulness to Him. I pray for Him to direct my thinking, my actions and to lead me to His will and not mine in every area of my life. Once I have prayed in that manner my day is so much better, and peace lives inside of me throughout the day. Whenever I start to have old thoughts again, try to control others or feel myself getting pissed off because they are not doing what I want them to do, I pray again for God to remind me that I am powerless over other people and to help me do His will and not mine. I can't explain how prayer works but I'll tell you it works every time. Try it!

No matter how much you want people to change remember: YOU are the only one you can change. You can't Control others, you can only control YOUR REACTIONS to them.

Here is a tool you can use when people are not doing things "the way you think they should, and you are getting ready to ract to them, T. H.I.N.K. about it. Ask yourself is your reaction going to be:

T HOUGHTFUL

H ELPFUL

I NSPIRING

N ECESSARY or

K IND

If not, don't say anything at all. This will take practice because keeping your mouth shut when people are being jerks can sometimes be very diffiult. But ultimately you will feel the peace inside yourself from making this choice.

It's very easy to be kind to people we like. The principle of kindness is truly demonstrated when we are dealing with people we do not like and who are difficult. Rick Warren, author of "The Purpose Driven Life", calls some people EGR's, Extra Grace Required. Some people really need an extra dose of our patience, tolerance and kindness.

There is a very important book I think every person should read. It is called 'The Five Love Languages" by Dr. Gary Chapman. Nothing has helped me to understand the differences between people's love needs like his book has. After reading it, I came to understand that every single person has their own love language and if you don't speak to them in their language, they will not feel loved. You must figure out which of the five languages someone speaks and them speak it to them. I suggest you read the book and find out what language the people closest to you speak. You may want to read this book with them or give them a copy so they can learn yours too! Miracles happen when you speak someone's love language to them.

There many tools available that will help improve the relationships in your life so you can gain more peace and have more Love. Try a few in the upcoming Contrary Actions. They work.

Contrary Actions:

1.   Make a list of all your relationships and the things about other people you have tried to change. Now realize you are powerless over them, that you could never change them and you never will.

2.   Ask God to help you remove drama from your life and give you the strength to do His Will

3.   Whenever you are upset by someone say the 3 C's to yourself as often as you need to throughout the day. "I didn't cause it, I can't control it and I can't cure it."

4.   Practice these five important and powerful words: Let go and let God.

5.   Say the Serenity Prayer to attain peace and serenity in your life: <u>God grant me the serenity to accept the things I cannot change (everyone and everything else but me).</u>

the courage to change the things I can (me), and
the wisdom to know the difference.
Once you know the difference and accept it, life
changes immediately. You will no longer be at war
within yourself or with the world, .

6.   Try reacting to people in a loving way, especially,
      when they don't do or say things the way you would
      like them to.

7.   Try not making any comment at all when people
      aren't following your blueprint for life.

8.   When conflict arises: Walk out of the room.

9.   Make a conscious decision to change your behavior
      and not say a word.

10.   Try saying: "Maybe you are right."

11.   Try accepting people as they are. Accept whatever

is happening and go focus on God and yourself.

12.   Read and memorize the following passage on Acceptance from the Big Book of Alcoholics Annonymous. Say it to yourself whenever you are unhappy, in conflict or disturbed:

"Acceptance is the answer to all my problems today. "When I am disturbed, it is because I find some person, place, thing or situation -- some fact of my life-unnaceptable to me, and I can find no serenity until I accept that person, place, thing or situation as being exactly the way it is supposed to be at this moment. Nothing, absolutely nothing, happens in God's world by mistake. Only when we learn to accept people as they are can we have serenity."

FOR ADVANCED WORK:

Object: Make a list of all of the behavior and actions you have taken that have negatively affected your relationships..Become conscious of your reactions to people so you can change them. .

Start by listing everyone you are mad at and why. Your list may include being ignored, being cheated on, not being listened to, being passed over for a promotion, etc. Break it up into 3 columns. COLUMN 1. Write down who are you mad at. COLUMN 2. Write down what did they do to you? After you are done with the 1st two columns label COLUMN 3 Call it MY REACTION and write down your reactions to each person for what they did to you.

EXAMPLES OF REACTIONS:

not communicating, ignoring someone, gossiping about them, holding things against them for years, not forgiving people, bringing up the past, lashing out verbally, insulting, withholding sex, them, making threats you don't intend to carry out, making judgements, rolling over and going to sleep. All these things are reactions people can have when we can't control what other people are doing. We feel powerless about it and we react hoping our behavior will somehow scare them, influence them, persuade them or intimidate them into doing what we want them to do. We are all guilty of this. Don't beat yourself up about it. Be gentle with yourself. God Loves you and nothing you have done has made you unlovable by God.

Now that you have completed these lists, put the first 2 columns out of your sight and focus only on the list of YOUR REACTIONS in COLUMN 3. This is the only thing within your power to change. You are responsible for not reacting like this anymore. No matter what people do, no matter how justified the anger. You are responsible to come from Love. What may be missing from your reaction list may be things like patience, tolerance, forgiveness and acceptance.

Also, notice how much time and energy you spend trying to control others. How little time we spend on taking care of ourselves, doing healthy actions.

Notice where we put our energy and remember what we put our energy into we get more of. If you put your energy today into the problem, you will get more of the problem. If you put your energy and focus into the solution: LOVE, you will get more of the solution. We create what we focus on.

CONGRATULATIONS!

I want to congratulate you if you did this exercise. It is very confrontational. I suggest you do this exercise every time a problem with someone arises. We have to train ourseleves to look at our part until it becomes a habit. People will never meet our expectations and we will always be disappointed in them to some degree. We must learn change our part, forgive them, and develop more patience and tolerance. <u>How can we expect the world to be more peaceful if we can't look at ourselves and be more peaceful and kind in our own lives?</u>

PART THREE

MY DIALOGUE WITH God

Contrary Action

Chapter 33
- See People for Who They Really Are!

"Disillusion adveho tantum ut illusioned. Unus cannot exsisto disillusioned of quis unus nunquam loco fides in."

"Disillusion comes only to the illusioned. One cannot be disillusioned of what one never put faith in."

Dorothy Thompson

14

One of the hardest things to do in relationships is to see people for who they really are and NOT who we want them to be.

When we first get into relationships with people we begin to realize on some level that they are not who we want them to be. However, often we keep holding on to them refusing to accept them the way they are. We spend so much time hoping people will change. We struggle with the idea of letting go, sometimes for years, refusing to be honest with ourselves about who the other person really is. Instead we believe in our own fantasies of that person.

When we realize someone is not good for us, or is not meeting our needs, we still hold on to them, hurting ourselves in the process. Where do we get the strength to cut people loose that don't Love us as God would Love us?

One way is by going into the silence and remembering who we really are and remembering our own tremendous value. We can remember that God wants the best for us, even in relationships. In fact, He has awesome plans for us and wants us to experience great joy and happiness in all areas of our lives. We need to turn to God to ask Him for direction in relationships and for the answers that show us the truth about the people in our lives. Then we must be courageous enough to receive the answers and accept them. Often the right thing to do is very hard to do. Removing toxic people from our lives is especially difficult.

Why are some of the hardest things to do ofetn the best things for us? Simply because the challenge of them builds character, and strengthens us. God designed life to strengthen us. Like a good workout, it does burn, but it builds muscle, too! Letting go of toxic people burns, but it builds muscle and the more we work that muscle the stronger we become, the better the choices we make, and the richer and fuller our lives become.

A woman I know named Ginger was dating a man named Randen and within the first few months of their courtship, he demanded she end her 13-year friendship with her ex husband of 10 years, saying he was not comfortable with her close friendship with him and couldn't accept it. She understood his feelings, but her ex was a big part of her family. They all Loved him and he was one of her best friends. Her ex was also in a new relationship with a beautiful woman whom he Loved and had children with. Their family was part of her family.

No matter how faithful Ginger was to Randen and even though she explained many times that her relationship with her ex husband was no threat to him, he couldn't accept it.

She tried to comfort him, include him in the relationship and make compromises, but Randen's insecurity and fear of losing Ginger was too great. They way he reacted when he felt inseucre was irratic, agressive and rude. His insecurity was a huge red flag for her, but she kept on trying to see him for she "hoped and thought" he was, rather than who he was. Ginger saw "potential" in him and kept trying to bring it out of him. It's been said that everyone has "potential" but that doesn't mean you have to marry them!

After 12 months of dating, Ginger was still trying to get Randen to accept her ex and it was a huge source of contention and hurtful behavior between them. One day Randen said to her the friendship with her ex was a deal breaker and "she wasn't worth it." They finally broke up, but only after causing each other a great deal of pain.

On reflection, Ginger was able see that Randen was a very self-centered, insecure man who couldn't get past his fears. His inability to trust was not a figment of her imagination. It was real, and denying it only prolonged the inevitable break-up. All her hoping he would change did nothing. She had become fixated on the fantasy of who she "hoped" he would be rather than accept the reality of who he really was.

Sometimes people would rather be with someone than no one. It takes courage to see people for who they really are. We don't do it initially because we are afraid we are going to lose out on Love, or there won't be anymore Love coming around for awhile. We have a false believe that Love is scarce. That's why we hold on as long as we do. But we are wrong. The truth is Love is abundant.

We can learn a lot from every relationship, even the ones that don't last. You can't marry potential. You can't change anyone except yourself. People will never fill the void within you, only God can. Each of us is worthy of relationships that are healthy. And each of us deserve people who are loving and accepting of who we are.

A good gauge for deciding whether you are in a good relationship or not s to imagine yourself in a relationship with God. What would that be like? How would He treat you, how would you be Loved? Knowing that people are never perfect, how close to that experience is your current relationship?

Contrary Actions:

1.   Stop kidding yourself. Start seeing your partner for who they are.

2.   Stop making demands that they be who you want them to be and start accepting them for who they are. You can either accept it, or you can't.

3.   If your partner is not who you really want, try to see if there is a way to compromise together on issues, finding some common ground. (Compromise means inventing something that has never existed before.) It means things won't be exactly the way you want them to be, or the way your partner does, but your compromise is satisfactory to both of you.

PART THREE

MY DIALOGUE WITH God

Contrary Action

Chapter 34
-   ## Five Things We Do To Destroy Relationships

"EGO don't vado down via of praedicatio."

"I don't go down the road of condemning."

Joel Osteen

---

1 Blame

Whenever a communication starts with blaming the other person you are already off on the wrong foot. Blame keeps you from looking at what you do and taking responsibility for it. It makes someone else the problem and not you. The only person you have power over is you so what you need to do is correct your flaws, even if someone else is wrong. I promise if there is a conflict, nine times out of ten you have done something to help create it. You may need to be more tolerant, forgiving, patient and kind. Your partner is your friend. Treat them as such.

Contrary Action:

1) Sit down with your partner and each of you list five things you do to enhance your relationship and five things you do to destroy it. Acknowledge each other's strengths and work on your own weaknesses. No more blame.

2 Bringing up the past

Not allowed. When you bring up the past, it is like adding kindling to the fire. You add more issues, more kindling, more logs, and you have a bigger fire. Stick with the issue at hand. You know the only reason you are bringing up old issues is to make your partner wrong and try to prove your case. You want to win. But if you win and your partner loses how is that good for your relationship? Isn't the purpose of a relationship supposed to be to create a supportive, nurturing, loving environment where each of you wins? The win/lose mentality has no place in a relationship and will only cause destruction to the fabulous opportunity you have to give and receive Love. I promise you if you have to be right, you will be right out of your relationship.

Contrary Action:

1) Never throw past issues into an current disagreement. If one of you does, take a time out and start the conversation again. Adults get time outs too!

3 Threats

Not allowed. Take a time out. When you feel heated and start saying things that are mean or you know you are going to regret, take a time out. Walk away for 15 minutes. Tell your partner when you will be back and take a break. Both of you need to unwind and relax. Physically the body takes 15 minutes to return to normal blood pressure and you need at least that much time to calm down. Once you get calm you'll be able to see things from a different perspective.

Come back together in 15 and if it still needs to be discussed try again in a kind and loving way. If it is not possible, save your issues for the following day. Set a specific time to discuss them. Hear each other out. Do not interrupt. Just listen. Ask your partner for what you want and need and respect them. They may or may not be able to meet your needs. Such is life. We can't always meet others needs and they can't always meet ours. You have to weigh it on a scale of importance.

Contrary Action:

1)   Ask yourself that if this week was your last week on earth would this issue really matter.

4 Communication

Here is one clue: While you are talking, you're not listening. If you aren't listening you are NOT communicating. Communication requires speaking AND listening. If one of these elements is missing there is no communication. Usually people are so busy thinking of what they are gong to say next they aren't even hearing what you are talking about at all. Also, not listening to the other person is disrespectful. What you or your partner say and feel is important. You may see things differently, but that does not ensure "rightness" People experience things differently and there are always two sides to every coin.

When a crime has witnesses, sometimes even the witnesses see the same situation differently. Perceptions vary in people. Your partner's perception will be different than yours, but guess what? They really may feel that way. You need to value your partner's feelings and thoughts. If you don't, why are you together? If you care about your partner both perceptions must matter. Listening to them doesn't mean you agree. But at least give them the respect to hear them out. Remember if one of you wins, the other loses.

Contrary Action:

1)	Try saying "Honey Maybe you are right."

5 Unrealistic Expectations

We so often expect our partners to surprise us and do something differently than the way they have done it repeatedly in the past. When you met them you knew there were things you didn't like and now that you are together you expect them to change. Unrealistic expectations. Relationships are about compromise. You can't change your partner. Don't even try. You are wasting your time. Getting mad at your partner for being exactly who you picked is not going to help.

Contrary Actions:

1) Write down five things about your partner you would like to change. Now throw out the list. Since YOU are the only one you can change, now write down five things about you and start changing those. Get on to the matters you can do something about: YOU.

2)   Write down five new ways of reacting to the behaviors or qualities you don't like in your partner. Practice one of YOUR new reactions next time they do one of those things on your list that you can't stand.

PART THREE

MY DIALOGUE WITH God
Contrary Action

Chapter 35
- Listen for the Question Mark

"Sepius distinctus inter a prosperitas matrimonium quod a mediocris unus consisto of decessio super three vel quattuor res a dies unsaid."

"Often the difference between a successful marriage and a mediocre one consists of leaving about three or four things a day unsaid."

Harlan Miller

One of the most important things I have learned in relationships and conversations with people is to listen for the question mark. What that means is when someone is talking to you, listen for the question mark at the end of their sentence. If you don't hear one they are not asking you a question so you don't have to say anything in response. It's not a question, it doesn't require an answer. You are just listening. This will require making a conscious choice to listen for the question mark and then be quiet if it isn't a question for you. If it is not a question you don't get to give your opinions, make statements, or anything else. You get to be quiet and listen.

You will see when people are talking that most of their sentences do not have a question mark at the end of them. Most relationships suffer because someone isn't listening. They are always trying to get their point in and be heard. Changing this one action can help you have less conflict and closer relationships.

Lets say for example that you are in a conversation with your mate, friend, or parent and they say to you "I don't like when you do blah, blah, blah, whatever it is. There is no question mark so you don't need to answer back with any comment. This prevents drama that escalates into an argument.

It is called listening. When most people hear a comment like: "I don't like when you do blah, blah, blah," they respond by getting defensive and sometimes retaliating with a comment about something they don't like about you, which causes an argument. The person making the statement didn't ask you a question. They didn't ask for a response. They were simply stating a feeling or thought that didn't require a response. Go try this. It is a new action you haven't taken before. When we do something we have never done, we will get something we never had. How about closer relationships. Is that something you want?

If you are having difficulty in any relationship begin listening for the question mark. I promise you things will change. It's a simple Action with powerful results. You will fall off the bike many times on this one, but it will be fun and as you get used to listening to the question mark. It will just become part of the way you communicate. People will appreciate you for it and you will feel better about yourself and more valued by others.

One mistake people make is when they want their lives to get better, they go to read a book about spiritual growth or improving their lives and when they close the book they expect there to be change. That is not how it works. You must take actions in order to experience change.

As I told you when you first started reading, this is a book about Actions. You must put these concepts into practice, and you can do it. I did.

Often we read something and say, yeah, that's the way I should be living, or, wouldn't that be great if I could live like that, or be like that, and then we put the book down and go about our business as usual. Of course, nothing changes. Do you know why? Because if nothing changes, nothing changes. Read that sentence again. It makes sense doesn't it?

Here is one quick and easy sentence you can write on your mirror and look at it every day: Change = Action. Change your actions, then your thinking will change. Sometimes the answer is so simple we don't even see it. You don't even have to do big actions. Just simple ones can cause substantial change.

HOW TO WORK THIS BOOK

This book is full off Action step you can take. Take these small, manageable actions consistently over time to produce great change in your life. Do them to become a better version of yourself, the person you truly long to be. As you read this book, pick one Contrary Action and begin to practice it. You will get good at it and it will become part of

who you are. It can take a month, a year, two years whatever. However long it takes is fine, but really pay attention
to applying this practice in your life. We can't master every
Concept at once, but we can master one at a time.

As you go on reading pick another Contrary Action
and practice it. After you have read the book, go back and
pick another Contrary Action and practice it. You can use
the book for years to help you become the person you really
want to be. Taking new actions and practicing the Contrary Actions will change your life for the better.

This is so important it bears repeating: If we want
our life to change, we must change our actions first. Change
your Actions and it will change how you feel about yourself,
others and the world around you. It does NOT work the
other way. You CANNOT wait until you feel better to take
an Action, you must take an Action in order to feel better.
This is a simple, basic principle you must undesrtand an
accept. Changing your life means changing your actions
one at a time.

Contrary Actions:

1)   Listen for the Question Mark. If there isn't one at
        the end of sentence, be quiet!

PART THREE

MY DIALOGUE WITH God

Contrary Action

Chapter 36

Setting Boundaries

EGO duco orbis quod sanctus fines finium super mihi fewer quod fewer escendo me sursum superus quod superus mountains.

"I draw circles and sacred boundaries about me; fewer and fewer climb with me up higher and higher mountains.

Friedrich Nietzsche

Boundaries. When we set them they are very powerful in protecting ourselves from the abusive actions of others. We don't learn much about boundaries in school or anywhere else but they are a very powerful tool. Often we don't set boundaries because we are afraid of hurting other people's feelings. However, we must set boundaries with people to teach them how we want to be treated. We can let them know what we will or will not tolerate or accept in our lives. If people can't respect our boundaries then they don't get the pleasure of our time or company. When we don't set boundaries we often endure toxic conversation, circumstances and situations.

Once when I was in college, I tried to gossip about my roommate to her cousin who was visiting from Ireland My roommate did something I didn't like and I wanted to complain about it to her cousin. When I started to go into the story the cousin said, "I'm not going to listen to that. If you have a problem with her you should tell her yourself." I was shocked at first, to say the least and then I continued again to try to make my point. She again said she didn't want to hear it and would not have that conversation with me. She didn't get angry, she said it very kindly. She simply asserted her boundary.

I was impressed. By setting her boundaries I learned

that she was not someone I could gossip with. I had to respect her for that and she taught me about the power of boundaries.

Setting boundaries in our relationships keeps a lot of unexpected and unpleasant events from happening. People know where you stand and know what the consequences are if they cross the line. Always remember, you are responsible for teaching people how to treat you. Personal power is so important. Anthony Robbins talks about it all the time. We have the power to say no and say yes, to allow people to urt us or not. If someone is abusive towards us we have the power to walk away and stay away from that person. If that person is a parent we have the right to say, "I will not allow you to treat me that way. I refuse to be around you unless you can speak to me in a kind manner."

I often get asked questions like: "My parents want me to come home and spend the Thanksgiving holiday with them, but when I am there all they do is argue and say mean things to me or my wife. They also want us to stay with them at their house for five days. Should I go?" I say to this: Are you crazy? No you don't have to stay at their house for five days. Get a hotel. Limit the visit to two days, set a boundary before you go that if any of the above takes place you are leaving, and then if it happens, leave.

You have the right to say no to people who are doing things you don't want done to you. I won't be around people who don't respect me or relate to me in a oving way. Often when people realize you are not a doormat they stop walking all over you. As for those stubborn people who never learn to respect your boundaries, sometimes the boundary has to be you just won't put yourself in certain situations with certain people, because you know they won't respect you or your boundaries.

If you are one of those people who over commits themselves trying to make everybody happy, or are afraid to say no because that may make people not like you, you need to practice setting boundaries. First of all, not everyone is going to like you, so get over it. Second running yourself ragged and not taking care of yourself emotionally, physically or spiritually is unhealthy. This can wear you down and then you'll be no good to anyone.

Here is a new idea for you. "NO" is a complete sentence. It starts with NO and it ends with NO. You do not need to explain yourself or do things that are harmful to you in order to try and please other people. When someone asks you to do something you feel uncomfortable doing, say NO.

Also some people have the habit of forcing their

needs onto others. When people try to force themselves on you, you have the right to say no, you have the right to take your time to think about their request and decide what is right for you. When someone asks you a question or tries to demand an answer from you right there on the spot, simply say "I'll get back to you on that." Then take time to think about what you really want to do.

For example, you bump into a friend and she asks you to babysit for her on Friday. Don't jump in with a yes just to please her in hopes that she will like you, or this will win you points. Tell her "I'll get back to you." Then take the issue home, look at your calendar, check with your husband or whomever, decide if that is what you want to do with your Friday night. You have the right to not have your time dictated to you, and the right to make choices and to be able to respond with answers that reflect your own needs. If you are going to say no, when you call her you can simply say: "I am not able to do that Friday night, some other time would be lovely." You do not owe any explanation.

When people ignore your NO and try to push you or guilt you into action, simply repeat the sentence to them: They obviously didn't hear you the first time. This may sound ridiculous but sometimes you may have to repeat the exact same sentence 3 or 4 times before people actually hear what you are saying. They are so busy trying to manipulate you into getting what they want that they aren't listening to you. People are funny that way.

Setting boundaries are ways of taking care of ourselves. That is crucial if we are ever able to take care of others. How can you teach your children to Love and care for themselves if you haven't even learned to do it for yourself? I believe there are certain things missing in our school system that weren't taught to us and aren't being taught to our children outside of school. Boundaries is one of them. Ther are others: Patience, Forgiveness, Kindness, Tolerance, Self Love, How to listen, Love of others, Respect, How to be of service to others, How to communicate, Self sacrifice, Effective communication, Boundaries, Kind loving communication, Healthy relationship skills, How to be a good friend, How to respect our differences, Giving, Being considerate, Choices and consequences, Being part of a team, Choosing healthy partners in relationships, Being our best, Denial, Red flags. Whew! But students sure know their ABC's and 1,2,3's.

I will simply say the educational system spends the majority of it's time on history, english and math and so little time on how to live life successfully, it scares me. No wonder we live in a country and world with such declining morals, increasing divorce rates, teenage murders, unwanted pregnancy, child abuse, etc. We should teach our children how to read and write and do arithmetic but we should also teach them how to live healthy, powerful, conscious, loving lives.

We are so blessed to have been given life on this beautiful planet. We should all remember to thank God daily for the privilege to be alive and remain in awe of the miracle life is. If this book is of any help to you in making your journey easier I am happy I have done something worthwhile. Keep growing. I know I am.

Contrary Actions:

1. Use the phrase I'll get back to you."

2. Use "No" as a complete sentence.

3

PART THREE

MY DIALOGUE WITH God

Contrary Action

Chapter 37

- ## Choosing A Partner Worthy of You

EGO have philologus ut tantum duos res es necesse ut servo one's uxor gauisus. Primoris , permissum suus reputo she's having suus own via. Quod secundus , permissum suus have is."

"I have learned that only two things are necessary to keep one's wife happy. First, let her think she's having her own way. And second, let her have it."

Lyndon B. Johnson

It's so important to get to know someone before you get in a relationship with them. Often we think of it backwards. We get romantic, passionate, and sexual and then check to see if this person really has the qualities we are looking for. Healthy, happy and successful relationships are done in the reverse.

Get to know the person first, their character, thoughts, how they live their lives, their actions, behaviors, goals, how they handle stress, challenges, how they deal with people, their families, etc. See if this is a person you can respect and if you really like who they are. This way you are hooking up with someone you really can build a foundation with.

Red flags are there for a reason, to protect and steer you away from people you are unlikely going to be able to build a relationship with. However, we often minimize red flags, ignore them, justify them and then wonder why the relationship didn't work out? We hold on to relationships for the sex, romance and the passion but over time those red flags become exactly the reasons our relationships don't turn out. No amount of Sex can hold a relationship together once reality sets in. In fact once reality sets in, sex often stops.

Many times we meet someone we are attracted to for

aesthetic reasons, surface qualities and then jump into a relationship too fast, too soon. We end up in painful situations that always end badly and are emotionally traumatic.

As I continue to grow spiritually I made a decision to live a conscious life. I no longer end up in relationships and say "how did I get here?" I no longer make choices that are based in denial, lack of reality or unrealistic expectations. I want to know if the person I am getting involved with really is a person I will respect and admire. Especially if I am going to bring children into this world with them. If I choose to contribute children to the planet I am responsible for contributing healthy ones who can contribute to the world. Not messed up kids who take away from it. I made a decision that if a man I date is not someone truly worthy of the God in me, then I would prefer to be alone. Of course, after I made that choice I met the most wonderful man ever.

I suggest that in order to live a "conscious life," and choose people who are healthy and good for us that we need to step back and get to know them before we become intimate with them. See if they are worthy of being in a relationship with. After all we are going to be spending our precious God-given time with these people. We don't want to spend it with just anybody.

Think about it. Before we buy a '

foundation, the roof, the plumbing, the ᴖ

for termites, mold or anything else that woᴜ

chasing the home a mistake. But we spend very lıᴜ

investigating the person we are going to have in our spaᴖ

our bed, our lives, and possibly even have children with.

We give more value to a house than to ourselves. The foun-

dation of a relationship is so important. It must be built on

solid ground, not sand or it will sink.

Contrary Actions:

1)   Make a list of the characteristics you want in a

    partner. Be specific. I had 102 items on my list.

    (My husband is 100 of them!)

2)   Don't settle for less than you truly want."

3

PART THREE

MY DIALOGUE WITH God

Contrary Action

Chapter 38

- Forgiveness

"EGO can indulgeo , tamen EGO cannot alieno , est tantum alius via of sententia , EGO mos non indulgeo. Venia ought ut exsisto amo a cancelled nota lacer in duos , quod exuro sursum , ut is nunquam can exsisto ostendo obviam unus."

I can forgive, but I cannot forget, is only another way of saying, I will not forgive. Forgiveness ought to be like a cancelled note - torn in two, and burned up, so that it never can be shown against one."

Henry Ward Beecher

Biblical parables teach many important lessons. Matthew 18:23-35 coontains the "Parable of the Unmericful Debtor" in which Jesus explains the meaning of forgiveness. HE likened the Kingdom of God unto a king who, in looking over his accounts, discovered that one of his servants owed him a large amount of money. The king was about to foreclose on this obligation and sell the man, his wife and his family into slavery for payment of the debt. But the servant besought him to have patience. So, moved with compassion, the king forgave him his debt.

If that were the end of the story it would imply we can take without giving, that there is a one-sided relationship with the universe. And this would not be just. Justice the balance of action and equal reaction, would not be maintained. The law of cause and effect, which runs through everything, would be violated.

The servant who had been forgiven went out rejoicing. On his way he met one who owed him a small amount of money, which he was unable to pay back. The one who had been forgiven would not forgive, he would not wait until the obligation could be fulfilled. He cast the one who owed him into prison.

Friends of the one cast into prison came and told their king what had been done. The lack of compassion of him who had been forgiven, but who refused to forgive others, caused the king to become angry. He commanded that the unmerciful servant be cast into prison until his own debt be paid. This story is a lesson to teach us that it is impossible to be forgiven, unless we forgive. We cannot receive what we refuse to give.

Forgiveness is a powerful tool, when used, can cause great love and healing. Not only in our relationships with others but in our relationship to ourselves. Yes, we all have hurts and have been wronged by others. Some tragically. The question is, in the face of that reality, "how much should we forgive?" Ernest Holmes answers the question-most profoundly in his book "Words that Heal," he says, "we must forgive until there is nothing left to forgive."

You have heard of the saying forgiveness is for you, not them. But I believe it is for both. Some believe holding on to anger and resentment can cause physical malady. In Mattthew 9:2 the Bible tells of a man sick of the palsy who was brought before Jesus. HE said: "Son be of good cheer, thy sins be forgiven thee. Arise, take up thy bed, and go unto thine house." It is now known that before the original flow of life can be restored any sense of guilt which obstructs this flow must be removed. Jesus knew the palsied man was suffering from a burden of guilt. The particular block which he removed was a subjective sense of self condemnation. It was guilt that caused his disease.

Jesus, as was his habit, went immediately to the focal point of the disturbance. He told the man that his sins were forgiven. He knew that all our troubles are tied back into, and spring from, a wrong relationship with the universe. Our inability to forgive others block us. Our inability to forgive ourselves provides an equal block that makes us feel we cannot be forgiven until we have forgiven others.

When we hold on to the energies of emotional pain, resentment towards others, and the common disappointment we feel when our expectations of others are not met, we end up creating dis-ease in the body. Letting that energy dissolve by establishing peace and harmony with people can create great health within our bodies. Often we can restore our health merely by the way we choose to look at things.

Often we are carrying around anger from experiences that have long since passed and are no longer happening. Yet, the anger is still happening inside our bodies. It is our decision whether or not to release this anger and let it go. Things happen that we don't like. People act in ways we don't like. But we can not change that. We can accept that exactly as it is even if we don't like it, and move on. It's called embracing reality.

If you get hit by a door, and, it cuts your head open, you don't like it. It hurts. You're wounded. You're bleeding. But you can't deny the door hit you. Yelling at the door for hitting you won't erase your cut. Wishing the door had never hit you won't undo the damage. Being angry for years that the door hit you is wasted energy. You have to accept that it happened, perhaps not like it, but move on.

We absolutely have to do that when people do or say things to us that we don't like or that are hurtful. We must accept that they did that and move on. Let go of the blame, let go of the whys? Let go of the anger and just move on. People make the mistake of holding on to that moment and the anger will cause dis-ease and sickness in the body. Forgiveness is mostly for you. Not for them. Revenge taste sweet at first, but is bitter over the long run. Forgiveness tastes bitter at first, but over the long run is a soothing, healing, balm.

Forgiveness takes place within your mind and body. Forgiveness is a tool for maintaining your own health. Use it often. I believe it is what God meant in the Bible when he said PHYSICIAN HEAL THYSELF. We can all use forgiveness as a tool to heal ourselves. It is magical.

Don't take things personally. This is so important

Don Miguel Ruiz. Ruiz wrote a terrific book about it called "The Four Agreements." If you have a chance you should read it and practice the principles he mentions.

I try not to take things personally. Rather, I try to experience life in each moment of living. Living in the present will keep us from living in the past or holding on to painful memories. If you observe the things people say and do and take none of those things personally, you would simply be un-affected, left in your original state. The state of perfection that God created you in.

When you take things personally you absorb another person's negative energy and internalize it. Your reactions or misconceived perception of what they do alter your physical and emotional state. Try letting what people outside of you say stay outside of you. Try letting people have no affect on you whatsoever. Say to yourself that what ever they do or say, that is them, it has nothing to do with me. It demonstrates who they are, not me.

I am not responsible for other people's emotions and feelings. I use this as a mantra, saying it over and over again, whenever I want to remain unscathed by people's negative energy. I say it to remind myself of the truth: That we are all one and acting from Love is all that matters. I try to stay focused on God's Will for me, God's Love for me and God's peace. When I say God's Will I mean remaining in LOVE. This level of conscious choice takes discipline and focus.

We are responsible for what we place our attention on. It is easy to get caught up in other people's drama or negativity, such as, gossip, the news media, people who feel sorry for themselves etc. When we meet people who are unhappy or angry we don't cause it. It is within them already because they aren't following God's Will for them. God's Will is to come from Love, and to have joy, peace, and happiness in our lives.

Sometimes our actions or words aggravate others, but it only aggravates an anger that already exists within them. You are not the cause of the anger. Don't let anyone blame you for their feelings or give you that much power.

You have heard many times that what we focus on we become. If we focus on other people's negative feelings or opinions of us, we will become filled with doubt and insecurity. If we focus on God's Love for us and his promise of peace and joy by following His Will, we become who we are intended to be. If we intend to be negative, we will be negative. If we intend to be positive we will be positive. We must therefore carefully decide what our intention is going to be in every moment. This may seem difficult to do at first, just like walking or riding a bike, but eventually this becomes second nature to us. Unfortunately, it is not something we are usually taught to do.

When people do things to us that are hurtful we must remember we are all spiritually sick, when we are not connected to God and our higher self. We must therefore treat them like we would treat any sick friend and show them patience, tolerance and compassion. We must offer the grace of forgiveness.

Here is a quick story about former President Jimm Carter and First Lady Rosalyn Carter. President Carter decided that he would never let another day end with Rosylyn or himself angry with the other. So he went out to his wood shop and cut a thin piece of walnut, a little smaller than a bank check. He carved on it the words, "Each evening forever this is good for an apology or forgiveness, as you desire." He gave the plaque to his wife. With his plaque, President Carter created an atmosphere of forgiveness between them. Without knowledge that we will be forgiven how quickly will we admit our faults? And how can our closest relationships be healthy if we are afraid to admit mistakes, apologize, or are unwilling to accept an apology. A climate of forgiveness is a necessary part of happiness.

Contrary Actions:

1) Look in the mirror every day and say this to yourself 5 times "I am independent of the good or bad
   opinions of others." Or "I am not responsible for
   other people emotions and feelings."

2) Read "The Four Agreements" by Don Miguel Ruiz.

3) Make a list of people you are angry with. Write
   down what they did to you and deliberately forgive
   them. It may be someone you have been holding a
   resentment towards for years. Your lack of forgiveness blocks the energy of life and health in your
   own body. Let it go now!.

4) Forgive yourself for something you have done.

5) Cut your spouse some slack. Carve them a plaque.

PART THREE

MY DIALOGUE WITH God

Contrary Action

Chapter 39

- How Can I Be More Loving?

"Sumo Lacuna ut constructim pontus quinymo quam molior barriers."

"Choose words that build bridges, rather than erect barriers."

Unknown

If you are thinking about whether or not to take an action you can ask yourself the question "what would Love do?" Or as Tina Turner would say, "what's love got to do, got to do with it?" If it is not the loving thing, don't do it. If it's not the loving thing to say, don't say it. Yes, I know it feels good sometimes to just tell someone like it is. But is that loving? Yes you may be right, but is that loving? Another way to decide if you should act or say something is to think of the highest version of yourself and ask yourself "would the highest version of myself do or say that?"

One of my biggest challenges is NOT saying what I think all the time. I believe in telling it like it is, but not everything that is thought needs to be expressed. Not everybody can handle the truth. And frankly, most people would rather die than hear the truth about their lives or themseleves. The truth can be a scary thing for people.

If you are about to take an action or say something, negative STOP. Take a step back, take a deep breath, or a few minutes to think. What would your highest self do? Then take that action. You will only regret acting from the lower part of yourself because you have to live with the guilt of your actions. When you act hurtfully or selfishly towards others you cut off your connection to God and to other people. You live with that loneliness inside you.

We are not perfect beings so there may be times that you say something you regret, that you know is not loving. Clean it up right away. Don't wait. Call that person, or send them a note, but apologize for your actions immediately. This takes practice and so does not mentioning their behaviors. Not allowed. An apology from you is not a call to blame them. Remember, you are there to clean up your actions and YOUR actions only. You are trying to come from Love and be the best YOU can be.

Sometimes, when you apologize first, people see your humility and often step up to the plate with an apology of their own. But that is not the reason you are apologizing.

If you are looking at your life and have decided you want to become conscious of your actions and more loving, I commend you. The world needs more people like you. To come from a truly loving place as often as you can will take work. You will definitely need to exercise your spiritual muscles. I still have to work at it when someone pushes my buttons, but now it is much easier and happens much quicker. I feel uncomfortable not being loving. I have changed considerably. I chose to.

It will take practice for your new actions to become new habits, so be gentle with yourself. Here are a few tools to help you grow.

Contrary Actions:

1)   Go to 3 or 4 people and ask them to write down the good qualities they see in you. *For example; thoughtful, resourceful, kind, full of life, affection- ate, honest.* Take their lists and compile then into one document. These are the qualities of your higher self. Place the list where you can always see it. Review the list everyday or whenever you need to be reminded of who you really are. When faced with challenging situations ask yourself:

2)   What would the person on my list do?

3)   Who would God have me be in this situation?

4)   What would God have me do in this situation?

5)   Or simply, what would Love do?

PART THREE

MY DIALOGUE WITH God

Contrary Action

Chapter 40
- ## Conclusion - LEAD ME HOME

"Ut quinque voluntas quod mens es etiam, quod causa intellect sileo in silentium, tunc suscipio altissimus semita."

"When the five senses and the mind are still, and the reasoning intellect rests in silence, then begins the highest path."

Katha Upanishad, 6

That's all I have to share with you about my journey, so far. It is not complete. I am always growing in God. But I've come a long way and you can make the journey too. I know somewhere inside you is a nagging feeling that there is something more. Something more that you are doing, something more than you are being. We all have it, because inside every Man, Woman and Child is the fundamental idea of God. You long for answers and a deeper connection with the divine. You can have it. Ask yourself this question: Do you want to know God more intimately?

If the answer is Yes, tell Him. Tell Him in any style you want. Tell Him in your heart, out loud, in writing, however you need. Cry to Him and ask Him directly to show you the truth about Him. Tell Him you want to know Him. Desire it in your heart. Remember, the bible says "God will give you the desires of your heart." If you desire it in your heart, and ask, God will answer you. He will reveal Himself to you. Just like he did to me. Not only to people like Mother Theresa, but to everyone, equally.

If you desire only earthly pleasures in your heart you will experience them, but they may only lead to pain, suffering, and disappointment. They will never fill the emptiness in your heart in the way that only the awareness of

the presence of God can fill. You already know that. You've
tried everything else and you still feel empty. You've tried
sports, careers, jobs, friends, activities, people, relationships, and children. It hasn't worked. You can search your
entire life outside you, but only with God will you find the
answers. Your answers. On my CD "As I Am " I sing a song
called LEAD ME HOME that was written by the wonderful
songwriter Phil McKenna that expresses what happened
to me:

> LEAD ME HOME
>
> "A quiet peace fell over me
>
> When I looked up and you were there
>
> You took a heart, afraid to speak
>
> And taught it words that we can share
>
> The child locked inside
>
> All the pain I tried to hide
>
> I couldn't see the love in me
>
> Without You as my Guide"

Thank you God For loving me. I pray that by reading
this book you realize how much God loves you too. There
are a series of Holy writings called the Upanishads, which
have a name that suggests "sitting at the feet of the Teacher." The earliest of the Upanishads date back some three

thousand years ago. In the Maitri Upanishad, VI.19-23 it is said; "when the mind is silent, beyond weakness and distraction, then it can enter into a world which is far beyond the mind: the supreme Destination. Then one knows the joy of Eternity."

The Bible says in Luke 17:20-21, the "Kingdom of Heaven is within You."If you don't go within, you will go without God.

The answers to all your questions and solutions for your life will be found in a personal one-on-one direct relationship with God. Forget what you have previously learned. Forget what people have told you. Forget the stupid things people have been done in the name of God that have made you doubt Him, or disbelieve His existence. Start fresh.

Get down on your knees, in silence, and go to Him directly. Not because you have an emergency and you need His help. Not because priests or your family, or society have forced you to in the past.

Go to God because you truly want to know Him better. Ask Him to show you the truth and be ready for the experience of your life, for you will truly be lead home.

If you ask – you shall receive. Namaste.